The Bitcoin Handbook

Key Concepts in Economics, Technology and Psychology

Edited by Anil Patel

Cover design by Anil Patel
Typesetting by artdesignbySF.com

Print and distribution by Konsensus Network

ISBN: 978-9916-697-98-6 (Hardcover)
978-9916-697-99-3 (Paperback)

Konsensus Network: https://konsensus.network
Publisher: info@konsensus.network
Author: anilsaidso@pm.me

To my children,

May you rightfully preserve the fruits
of your labor without sly impairment.

"Anil has done an incredible job visually illustrating some of the most important concepts in bitcoin in an intuitive, appealing, and popular way. His visuals capture the essence of important concepts in very simple illustrations that force you to think of them deeply."

Saifedean Ammous

Author, The Bitcoin Standard & Principles of Economics
Host, The Bitcoin Standard Podcast

"Bitcoin offers a lifeline to people around the world facing relentless inflation, political repression, and rampant corruption. However, education is crucial in reaching them. This book will hopefully play a role in that."

Alex Gladstein

Chief Strategy Officer, Human Rights Foundation
Author, Hidden Repression

"Anil has an impressive ability to condense down hundreds of hours of reading, listening and learning into simple graphics. Advancing bitcoin knowledge is the most important thing for spreading human liberty and flourishing."

Stephan Livera

Host, The Stephan Livera Podcast

"Like the masters at Marvel and DC Comics, Anil possesses the rare and powerful ability to combine words and imagery for incredibly effective communication, helping bitcoin signal to break through the noise."

Cory Klippsten

CEO, Swan Bitcoin

"Anil has a great way of condensing complex ideas into visual form that makes absorbing them much easier for the layperson."

Vijay Boyapati

Author, The Bullish Case for Bitcoin

"Anil's illustrations are stunningly beautiful and a testament to his deep understanding of the subject matter. It is a joy to see them compiled in a book."

Gigi

Author, 21 Lessons & 21 Ways
Founder, Einundzwanzig

"I love this. I will reference this on my shelf. The graphical design work is phenomenal. It lays out such focused and clean first-principles thinking on really complicated ideas, making them accessible."

Preston Pysh

Cofounder, The Investor's Podcast Network

"To me, The Bitcoin Handbook is special. Not only does it superbly summarize numerous critical concepts, but also it shows the author has a deep connection with the bitcoin community."

Tuur Demeester

Editor in Chief at Adamant Research

Anil Patel
@anilsaidso

CONTENTS

PREFACE

It may sound selfish, but I didn't write this book for you.

I wrote it for me.

Bitcoin is multifaceted and multidisciplinary. Comprehending it demands first-principles thinking.

I set out to acquire the broadest understanding of monetary technology and communication networks that my intelligence would permit in order to translate it into a single resource.

The process forced me to research, curate, and synthesize vast amounts of information. Many notepads were filled, with much ending up on the proverbial cutting-room floor. I obsessed over brevity, stripping away anything non-essential to seeing the bigger picture.

The result is a reference-style book that is concise, timeless, and defensible. While it can be consumed in a single sitting, I hope you'll stop to ponder the material, connecting it to unique experiences from your life. This is how understanding is cemented.

Should the table of contents appear daunting, rest assured that this book is free of jargon and unnecessary complexity (this author has no interest in sounding smart).

When applied in aggregate, this specific collection of concepts will best serve you (and me) in navigating a world of ever-accelerating change at the hands of technology.

Godspeed.

Nothing contained in this book should be construed as financial, tax, or legal advice.

FOREWORD BY JEFF BOOTH

Our frame of reference guides our thoughts, words, and actions which form our reality. We might not realize it, but we control our frame in that it is only us who can change it. Each of our own lives is a mirror reflection (with a time lag) of those thoughts, beliefs, and actions. Our society is formed by a shared reality of them. This is what creates the beautiful, unpredictable, and often chaotic mosaic of life.

Regularly, our frame doesn't achieve our desired results. Instead of looking critically at our own frame, we most often turn to those who will reinforce our own beliefs back to us, rarely discovering the magic of what may lay outside our frame.

If the reference frame in question was an economic system underlying all other emergent properties of our shared reality and every person within it, it would be disconcerting to say the least. Especially if our frame might be wrong. A system problem couldn't be solved by the system creating the problem, yet we would probably miss it by measuring through that system.

That is the rabbit hole of Bitcoin. A completely decentralized and secure emergent network that is outside of the existing system. For the open and curious, an almost endless path of learning through economics, game theory, energy, physics, technology, systems theory, philosophy, and psychology. And at the end of the rabbit hole, conviction by its growing legion of supporters on why it is so important for humanity. In turn, leading to why it is so polarizing for others who haven't yet taken the journey.

Different frames of the world competing for thoughts, words, and actions. A current frame for how the world is organized today: rooted in coercion, control and scarcity. And a new frame built on the emergent network that is Bitcoin: rooted in truth, hope and abundance.

You owe it to yourself to explore with an open mind to determine if you're in the right frame.

PART I:
Economics

SCARCITY

How limited resources are allocated and sought-after.

Scarce resources incite competition over their possession, reflected through price in a free market. Many previously scarce things are now abundant thanks to innovation (e.g, calories, textiles, information, etc.).

A commodity may become increasingly scarce if demand as an industrial input rises faster than new supply is produced. Conversely, money is typically chosen by the market as the most liquid and salable thing that's value is defended by its inherent scarcity.

"The first lesson of economics is scarcity: There is never enough of anything to satisfy all those who want it. The first lesson of politics is to disregard the first lesson of economics."

-THOMAS SOWELL

The property of scarcity in money provides the incentive to create abundance in other things, as it provides a mechanism to reliably store value.

Bitcoin represents the invention of digital scarcity in that we've never had an irreproducible and independently verifiable digital unit. Its fixed terminal supply, enforced by a novel decentralized consensus process, makes it absolutely scarce. And there is no level of scarcity beyond absolute scarcity.

RELATED CONCEPT

MONETARY PREMIUM

The additional value commanded by goods for their ability to perform the functions of money in addition to their other uses.

When the scarcity property of money is violated, its ability to reliably store value starts to break down.

Until a new form of money emerges, other scarce assets and resources fill this void in the market in the interim, attracting a monetary premium.

"When the dominant money becomes terminally ill, we witness the short-term monetization of everything else."

-TUUR DEMEESTER

Eventually, such monetary premiums get drained when a superior form of money (possessing more desirable monetary properties) arrives.

VIJAY BOYAPATI

"A characteristic that is common to all monetary goods is that their purchasing power is higher than can be justified by their use-value alone. Indeed, many historical monies had no use-value at all. The difference between the purchasing power of a monetary good and the exchange-value it could command for its inherent usefulness can be thought of as a 'monetary premium."

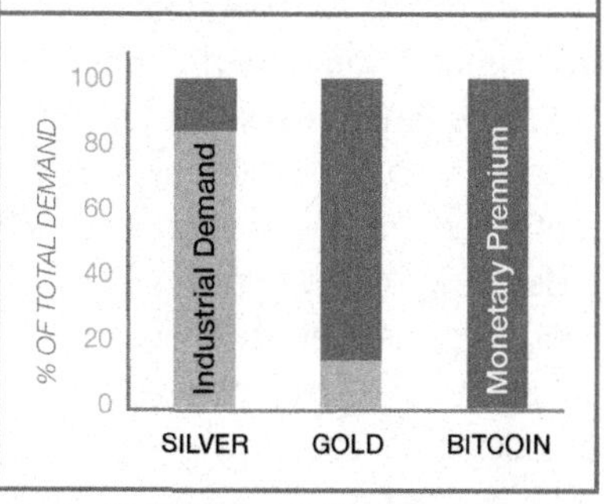

Source: 'The Bullish Case for Bitcoin' by Vijay Boyapati

GRESHAM'S LAW

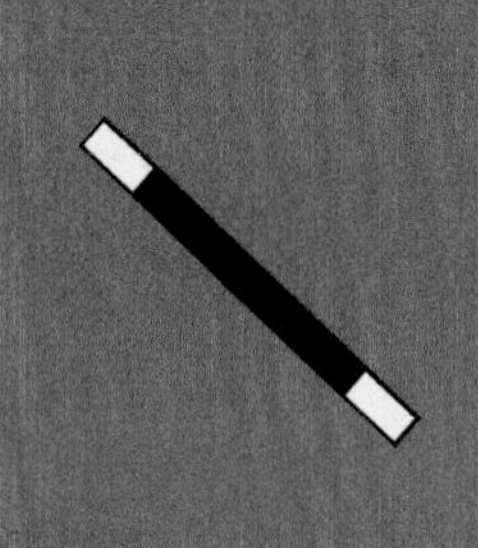

When two forms of commodity money are decreed with equivalent face value, the more valuable one disappears from circulation.

Gresham's Law explains how people rationally behave when the melt value of a commodity money drops below the face value, while circulating among versions of a higher purity, spending the former and saving the latter.

"Consistency, stability and high quality have been the attributes of great currencies that have won the competition for use as international money."

-ROBERT MUNDELL

While in service to Queen Elizabeth I, Gresham made the distinction between 'good' and 'bad' money at a time when precious metals circulated as money in Britain under Henry VIII. He noticed that the declining quality of new coins (lower precious metal content) resulted in older coins of a higher purity being saved.

A decline in the purity of coinage would predictably result in declining levels of trust in the issuer.

GRESHAM'S LAW

While this concept originated regarding physical commodity money, Gresham's Law can be applied to a fiat standard where debasement occurs via supply inflation.

With bitcoin now providing a competing monetary unit, with higher confidence in long-term wealth preservation, a natural trend is emerging of saving in bitcoin and spending down remaining fiat reserves.

"Standing by itself, the general statement, 'good money drives out bad,' is the more correct empirical proposition. Historically, it has been good, strong currencies that have driven out bad, weak currencies. The florins, ducats, and sequins of the Italian city-states did not become the 'dollars of the Middle Ages' because they were bad coins."

-ROBERT MUNDELL

RELATED CONCEPT THIERS' LAW

Absent legal tender laws, money that cannot be relied upon to preserve value will be rejected in favor of superior forms.

What if, instead of disappearing from circulation, the higher-quality form of money commanded a premium or the lower-quality form of money was rejected altogether by merchants?

Thiers' law assumes that legal tender laws attempting to enforce the use of an impaired form of money at a specific denominated value will go ignored at a certain threshold.

CANTILLON EFFECT

New units of money create disproportionate price inflation when added into an economy based on the path they travel.

Concerned with the path that newly minted money travels upon entering the economy, Cantillon posited that the initial recipients enjoy higher standards of living at the expense of later recipients. This is due to their unique spending preferences causing a disproportionate rise in prices (relative inflation) among goods in an economy.

Although Cantillon wrote in the context of commodity money (gold and silver), his point holds even greater relevance in the fiat era. Unconstrained money printing combined with suppressed interest rates has predictably seen asset prices soar, benefitting owners but also those with the greatest access to credit.

"No matter who obtains the new money.. It will more or less be directed to certain kinds of commodities or merchandise, according to the judgment of those who acquire the money. Market prices will increase more for certain goods than for others."

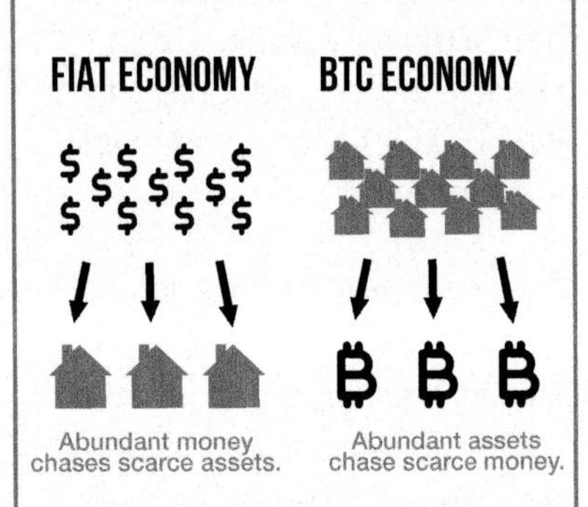

CANTILLON EFFECT

Bitcoin offers an antidote with its perfectly inelastic money supply. Purchasing power can not be reduced through dilution, and the lack of a central issuing authority means there is no one to lobby or co-opt.

"Money production.. redistributes real income from later to earlier owners of the new money."

-JÖRG GUIDO HÜLSMANN

A fiat monetary system with arbitrary price inflation targets also runs counter to the deflationary nature of technology, robbing society of gains in efficiency. Once this truth is understood, using fiat currency as a store of value ceases to be a viable long-term option. We can observe a small but steady migration of fiat users opting into bitcoin as trust in central planners continues to erode.

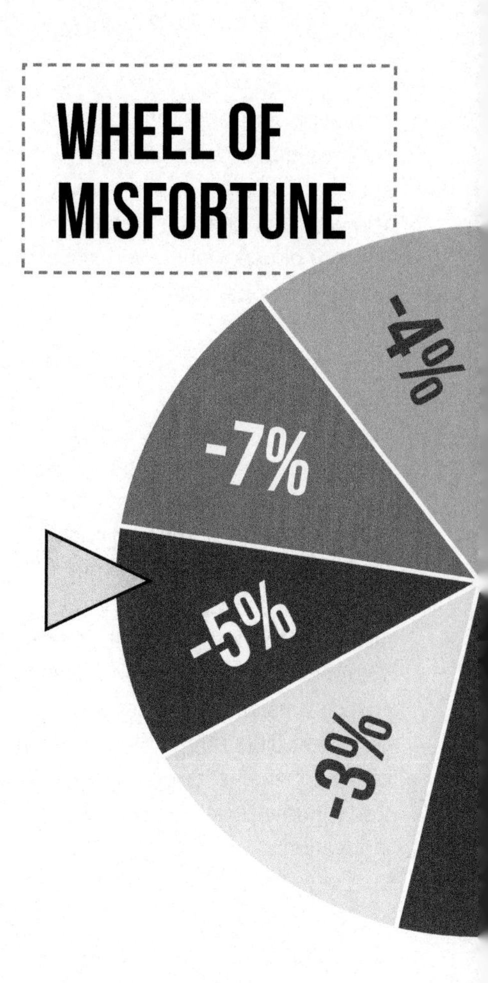

SCHELLING POINT

The solution that people choose by default in the absence of communication.

In multiplayer cooperative games, success depends on your ability to anticipate the choices of others. The wrong choice may result in facing a consequence or missing out on some benefit.

How we communicate with others follows a similar logic, as communication is just one big multiplayer cooperative game played with others in the same network. Standardizing protocols for communication (e.g., email, spoken language, money, etc.) allows us to most efficiently interact with the broadest possible range of participants with the least amount of friction. This brings many obvious benefits, such as increased trade, knowledge exchange, and innovation.

"Money facilitates social scalability by increasing the opportunities for..exchange."

-NICK SZABO

In the digital realm (absent legal tender laws), convergence will occur toward the money that most accurately communicates price signals, enabling coordination between market participants. This option becomes the default (Schelling point) over time as the expectation that others will also choose it grows.

THOMAS SCHELLING

"People are impinging on other people and adapting to other people. What people do affects what other people do."

SCHELLING POINT

Bitcoin is a protocol for exchanging value that has a crucial advantage over the fiat system—it features a terminal supply. Fiat currencies typically decline in purchasing power over time due to the incentives of the issuer to debase; all the while, bitcoin continues a decade-long march of increasing purchasing power in real terms.

Combining this with the immutability of the ledger and the benefits offered by the network (i.e., permissionless, global, and indestructible), bitcoin naturally becomes a monetary Schelling point.

$$\sum_{i=0}^{32} 210{,}000 \frac{50}{2^{i}}$$

OPPORTUNITY COST

When doing one thing comes at the cost of not being able to do something else.

Every financial decision is a trade-off with your future self. Bitcoin makes this abundantly clear on long timescales. As a superior method for long-term value storage (i.e., savings), bitcoin has established a new benchmark for investment decisions.

"When money is hard and can appreciate, individuals are likely to be very discerning about what they spend it on, as the opportunity cost appreciates over time."

-SAIFEDEAN AMMOUS

While bitcoin's annualized returns over the past decade have been eye-catching, they've only been captured by the holders who have forgone using that capital for other needs or opportunities as a result of conviction derived from first-principles thinking.

"Saving money in our MMT inflationary society is simply not an option. Everyone is either forced into investment or forced to watch their savings melt away."

-MORGEN ROCHARD

As the fiat system's pernicious design continues to push the burden of wealth preservation onto the individual, sound financial decisions have never held a greater significance.

RELATED CONCEPT

TIME PREFERENCE

The degree to which someone values the present relative to the future.

The time horizon we operate on affects the decisions we make. The degree to which we value the present relative to the future is known as time preference.

"Because humans do not live eternally...there is always a discount on the future compared to the present."

-SAIFEDEAN AMMOUS

Optimizing for the short term may equate to engaging in zero-sum games and seeking instant gratification, while optimizing for the long term may lead to delaying present consumption to invest resources in more productive activities for some expected future benefit.

Several factors influence one's time preference: personal safety, tax rates, property rights, the ability to reliably store value, etc.

The hardness of money across time plays a vital role in enabling and incentivizing individuals (and companies) to save, plan, and invest for the future. In a high-velocity fiat economy, access to credit is crucial, as short-term growth is rewarded over long-term profitability.

It's important to note that time preference is not a binary choice but a fluid spectrum. The incentives of your environment influence your actions, and your environment is constantly evolving.

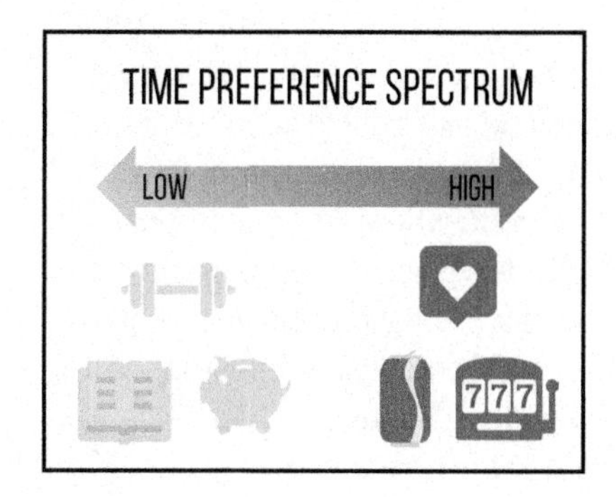

IMPOSSIBLE TRINITY

A sovereign nation cannot simultaneously have free capital flows, independent monetary policy and a fixed exchange rate.

The Impossible Trinity (also known as the Mundell-Fleming Trilemma) is a stark reminder to central planners of the trade-offs in setting international monetary policy. It states that sovereign nations can pursue only two of the following three options:

- Fixed Exchange Rates
- Free Capital Flows
- Independent Monetary Policy

While sovereign nations may wish to control and direct capital flows, they do not exist in isolation. Capital is increasingly mobile and will go to where it's treated best. Mundell's model (1963) assumed perfect capital mobility (although purely theoretical at the time) as it was the general direction he saw the world heading in.

"The international economic climate has changed in the direction of financial integration and this has important implications for economic policy."

Today, bitcoin is breathing new light into this theory. As a truly borderless and immutable technology for storing and transferring value, bitcoin is perfectly mobile capital. This fundamentally alters the logic and power of sovereign nations to direct international monetary policy.

IMPOSSIBLE TRINITY

"Currency pegs always break.
Free markets always win eventually.
It's just a question of when."

-CAITLIN LONG

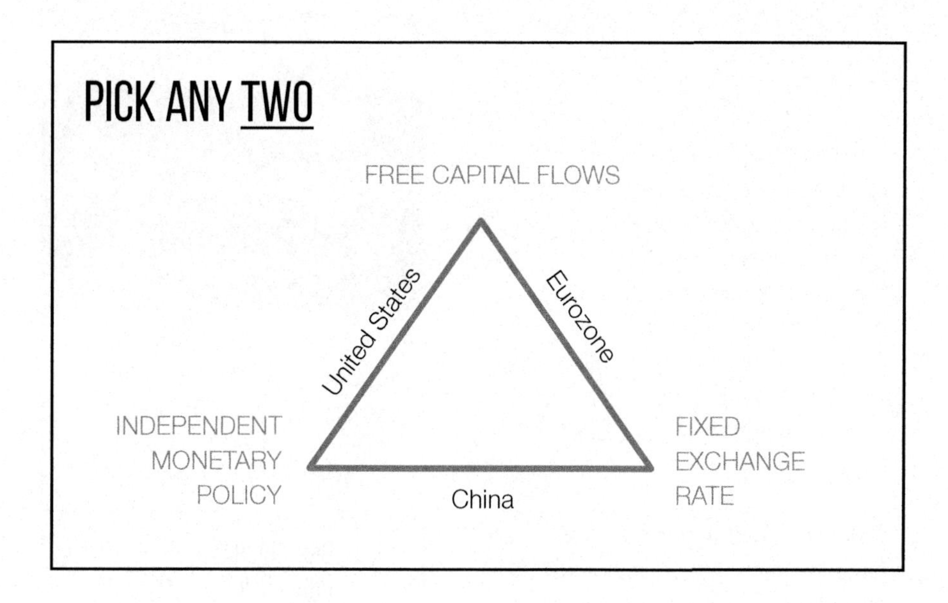

JEVONS PARADOX

The observation that consumption of a resource increases when efficiency gains are achieved through its use.

When a scarce resource becomes more abundant, we can expect to consume more of it due to declining costs. This may come from discovering new deposits or extraction methods, but it can also come from increasing the efficiency with which a resource is consumed (getting more out of the same input).

Gains in consumption efficiency have the same effect as increasing abundance- demand for the resource grows. This is Jevons paradox in a nutshell. Nowhere is this concept more apparent than in the context of energy resources.

In the late 1700s, the English public believed coal deposits were limited and depleting faster than they could be replenished. But, constraints breed innovation, and James Watt's steam engine would soon drastically expand coal's role as an energy input.

William Jevons pointed out the likely repercussions of Watt's steam engine in increasing coal demand. He would be proven correct in the coming decades as coal became indispensable in manufacturing, transportation, and even coal mining.

JEVONS PARADOX

"A fundamental fact of energetics, an impressive example of how every transition to a new form of energy supply has to be powered by the intensive deployment of existing energies and prime movers."

-VACLAV SMIL

The relationship between energy and money is undeniable and inescapable. Many people have proposed a money linked to energy throughout modern history as a method to remove centralized control and moral hazard from the equation. Still, none were able to design or implement it successfully. Enter Satoshi Nakamoto.

Bitcoin's proof of work consensus mechanism provides an economic incentive to harness energy resources in the most efficient manner available, as determined by the individual who bore the cost to acquire it.

While bitcoin's use of energy as a security mechanism is often a target of critics, much of the argument boils down to a premise in which all the world's available energy is known, limited, or finite. This assumes humans are incapable of innovating to increase the energy generated from a fuel source, which, as we know, is untrue.

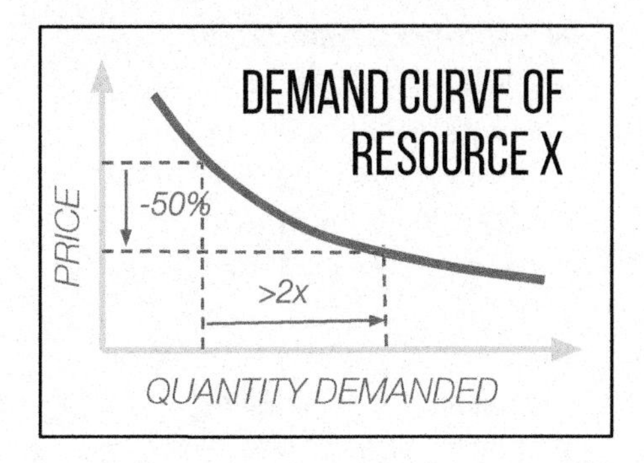

POWER LAWS

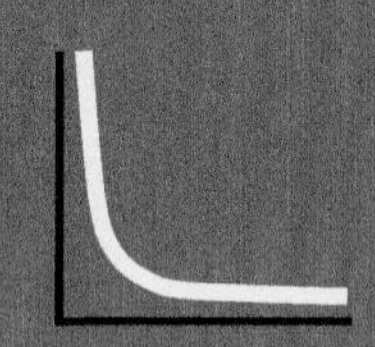

Relationships between two quantities, where changes to one lead to a disproportional relative change to the other.

Power laws can help to explain the correlation in certain nonlinear relationships and can be found across various fields, from linguistics to biology to astronomy. The basic idea is that small changes in one thing result in large changes to the other at a somewhat consistent rate.

In economics, power laws are often represented graphically as probability distributions. One of the most well-known examples is the Pareto principle (a.k.a. the 80/20 rule), where ~80% of outcomes can be attributed to 20% of inputs. Applying this principle to a market gives us a scenario where 20% of producers garner 80% of the market share, resulting in a long tail.

Similar distributions (while not strictly power laws) can be observed across various aspects of bitcoin: mining pools attracting hash power, hardware wallet sales across manufacturers, the distribution of bitcoin held across all addresses, etc.

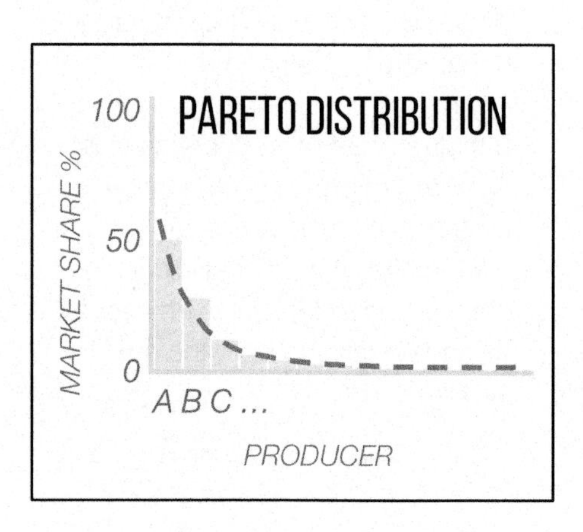

RELATED CONCEPT

WINNER-TAKE-ALL EFFECTS

A property of certain markets where minor advantages over competitors result in capturing all or most of the market.

Certain markets are winner-take-all competitions, where only the single most useful offering is required. In these situations, minor advantages in performance or value provided can result in capturing the entire pie.

"Money is a network. Some networks are singular, i.e. winner-takes-all. Money is such a network."

-GIGI

This occurs most notably when convergence toward a common standard offers users the greatest benefit, spurring network effects (see Schelling point).

Humans naturally gravitate toward using one common money within a defined region in a free market because it gives us the greatest optionality across the largest number of trading partners and offers the deepest liquidity. Unanimity is in our self-interest.

"Ultimately, monetary systems converge on one medium because their utility is liquidity.. And liquidity consolidates around the most secure, long-term store of value."

-PARKER LEWIS

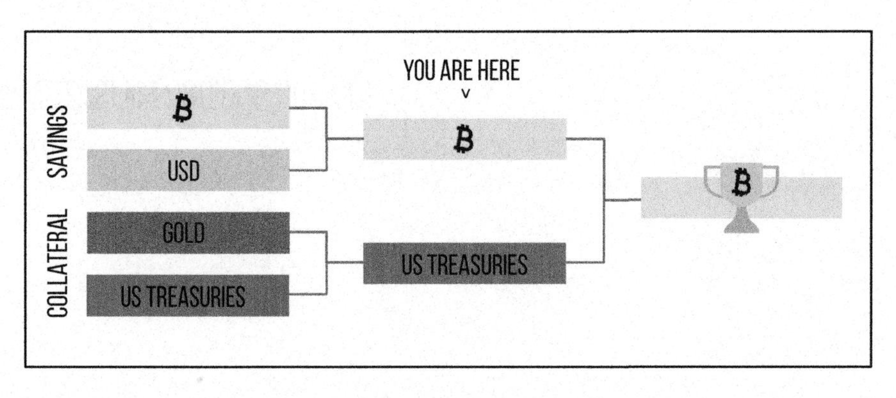

UNIT BIAS

The faulty reasoning that a single unit must be the appropriate amount from which to make assessments and comparisons.

Assessing bitcoin against competing stores of value based on unit price alone is illogical, as it fails to account for the total market capitalization (total units * unit price).

Much of this confusion arises from ignorance of bitcoin's current divisibility, down to eight decimal places (and 11 on the lightning network). As the maxim goes—you can buy a fraction of a bitcoin.

In reality, this level of granularity contributes to making it both desirable and practical as digital money.

"The desire to own a whole unit of a cryptocurrency leads many investors to mistakenly believe that competing cryptocurrencies are more affordable because individual units of those currencies have a lower price."

-VIJAY BOYAPATI

Satoshi Nakamoto's breakthrough innovation of digital scarcity means that holders own a non-dilutive share of a finite supply indefinitely. This cannot be said for any other store of value.

When viewed through this lens, bitcoin represents just a drop in the bucket when pitted against comparable asset classes and stores of wealth.

1.00000000 BITCOIN
=
100,000,000 SATOSHIS
=
100,000,000,000 MILISATOSHIS 

VEBLEN GOOD

Types of goods where the quantity demanded increases as the price increases.

When a person's income rises, they can spend more on goods. The type of goods that typically experience greater demand with wage increases (e.g., restaurants, electronics, vacations, etc.) are known as normal goods.

Conversely, Veblen goods are an economic anomaly in which demand increases as price increases. This label is commonly used to describe the behavioral psychology around some luxury goods, where a producer artificially constrains supply to manufacture scarcity.

While some future bitcoin demand may stem from its role as a status symbol, the likely dominant source will come from its absolute scarcity as a store of value. As demand for bitcoin increases, the price rises, creating deeper liquidity. As liquidity deepens, it enables larger market participants.

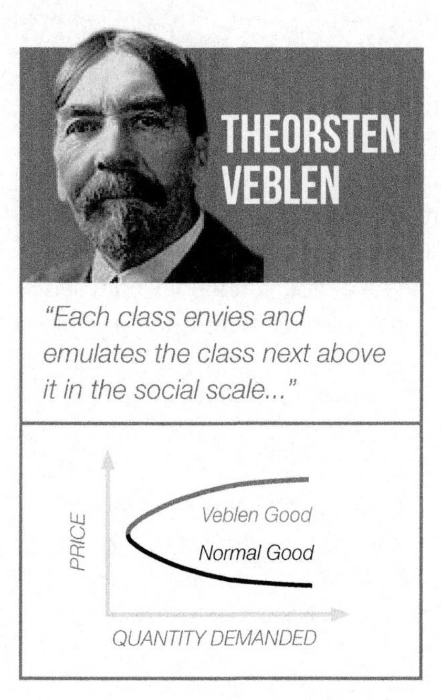

"Bitcoin demand increases as the price increases. Why? Because liquidity is a network effect and in Bitcoin's case there is no offsetting increase in supply."

-PIERRE ROCHARD

MALINVESTMENT

Distorted price signals cause a misallocation of capital towards less productive uses than would otherwise be chosen under a free market.

Long-term decisions inherently involve a degree of uncertainty. Hence, all investment decisions made today require making assumptions about the future. This can be a difficult undertaking when market forces are distorted and/or suppressed. It's like trying to use a compass when your point of reference keeps changing.

In a more practical sense, we can look at the phenomena of zombie companies (firms unable to meet interest payments on existing debt). Their survival is dependent on being able to refinancing at continually lower rates or additional borrowing. Hence, they are effectively walking dead.

"Government is deprived of a free price system and profit and-loss criteria, and can only blunder along, blindly 'investing' without being able to invest properly in the right fields, the right products, or the right places. A beautiful sub way will be built, but no wheels will be available for the trains; a giant dam, but no copper for transmission lines."

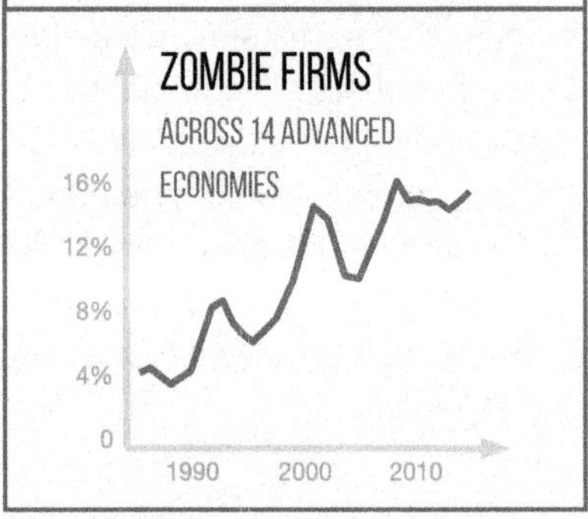

Source: Datastream Worldscope; Banerjee & Hoffman (BIS, 2020)

ASYMMETRIC PAYOFF

The disproportional upside of some investments, when compared to their downside risk.

When making an investment decision, we calculate the probabilities of the range of possible outcomes. In certain cases, the outcomes may be nonlinear, meaning the value of the investment changes such that it can increase proportionately more than decrease.

Bitcoin currently behaves a bit like an option, where the most likely outcomes are binary—it either succeeds or doesn't. In this sense, the downside risk is capped at zero (should it experience a catastrophic event). At the same time, its potential upside is orders of magnitude greater (bitcoin's total addressable market as the primary global store of wealth).

Asymmetry in payoff can only come as a result of asymmetry in information. If everyone properly understood bitcoin, it would already be fully monetized. Today, much of the world is yet to wake up to the superior monetary properties of bitcoin, and until then, upside potential will remain as a function of increasing demand pushing up against an inelastic supply.

"We can debate whether or not bitcoin is going to be a big deal in the future. But I don't think we can debate, that if it is, it's going to have an enormous right tail."

-ROSS STEVENS

ANSOFF MATRIX

A strategic framework for growth opportunities of a product across lines and markets.

Bitcoin's potential growth and total addressable market becomes clearer when thinking of it as a product (digitally-native hard money) serving multiple markets simultaneously. Ansoff's framework is a useful guide for this exercise. It outlines four alternative growth strategies for an organization in regards to developing a product and/or market:

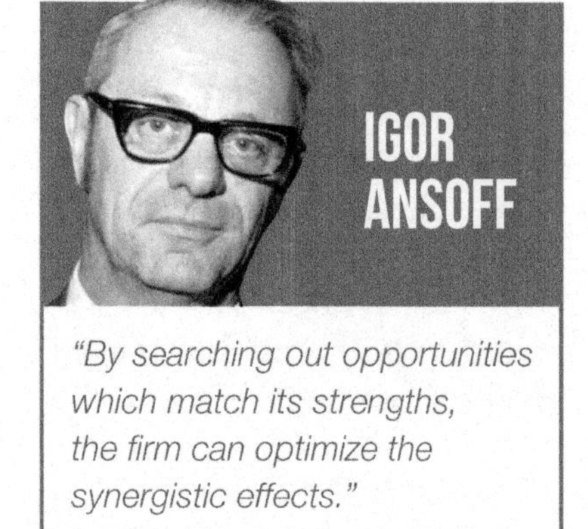

"By searching out opportunities which match its strengths, the firm can optimize the synergistic effects."

1. **Market Penetration:** increasing adoption/ saturation of an existing product in an existing market.

2. **Product Development:** launching a new product in an existing market.

3. **Market Development:** taking an existing product to a new market.

4. **Diversification:** launching a new product in a new market.

ANSOFF MATRIX

Bitcoin offers savings technology at scale and the lightning network offers payments technology for transacting bitcoin at scale.

One primarily protects your wealth from seizure, dilution, and censorship (competing with central banks and settlement networks). The other enables you to send and receive bitcoin micropayments anywhere in the world without verification requirements (competing with remittance providers, payment processors, and physical fiat currency).

For sound money to be productized under "bitcoin" as a recognizable brand is perhaps one of the least appreciated aspects of the adoption curve. Bitcoin not only has room to grow in terms of global saturation (horizontally) but also in terms of the allocation weighting within existing portfolios of both individuals and companies (vertically).

While an interest in inflation-resistant wealth may be a key driver of growth today, we should not underestimate new use cases and sources of demand for such a tool.

"Bitcoin enables novel financial use cases that were not possible before. This increases the size of the economic pie, thus generating wealth for society."

-BRANDON QUITTEM

PART II:
Technology & Systems

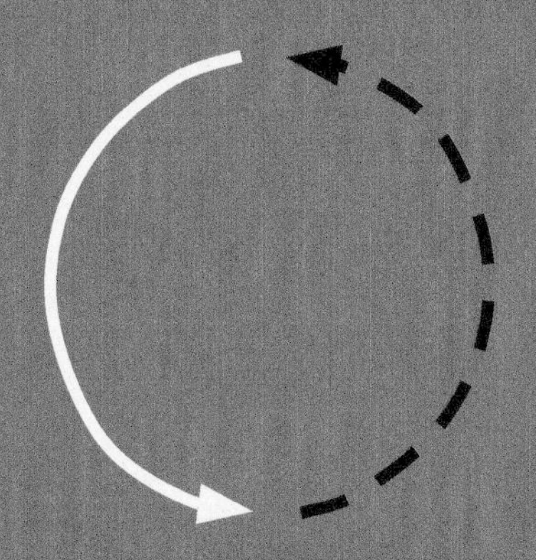

ORDERS OF MAGNITUDE

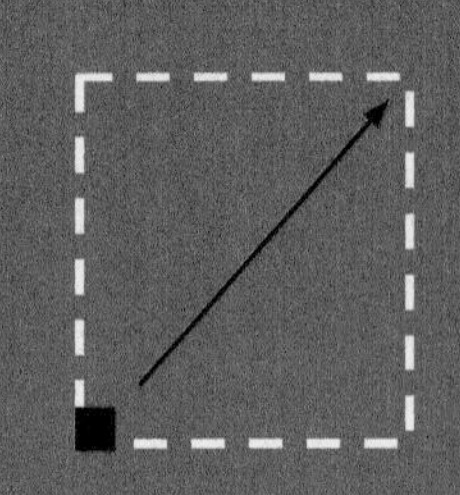

Representing numbers in a compact form of multiples of ten to make comparisons more intuitive.

Orders of magnitude are a helpful scale of measurement when analyzing the trajectory of fundamentally disruptive technologies and trends. Thinking in linear terms can fail to adequately capture the nature of exponential growth, often occurring in stages (see Gartner's hype cycle) depicted as a series of S-curves.

We can also use this tool to examine bitcoin's unit price over time (a measure of demand for bitcoin). Using log scale to see relative change, instead of linear scale (absolute changes), enables us to observe a noticeable long-term exponential trend.

This signifies that a permanent shift in monetary technology is underway.

"As adoption of a monetary network increases by an order of magnitude (10x), possible network connections increase by two orders of magnitude (100x)."

-PARKER LEWIS

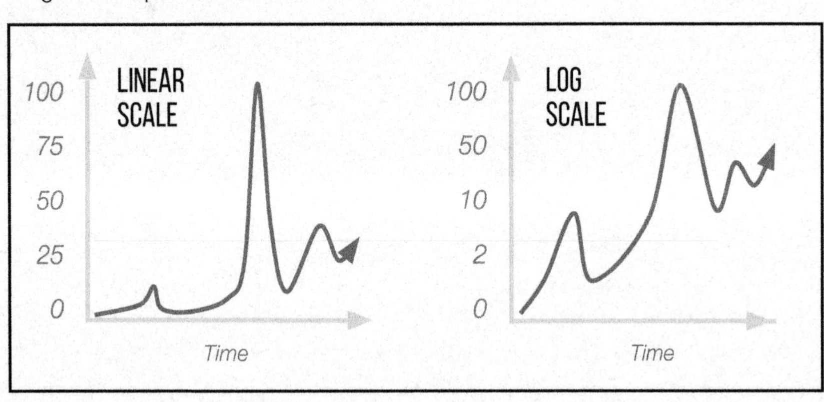

RELATED CONCEPT

10X IMPROVEMENT RULE

New technologies must offer a benefit ten times greater than a predecessor or substitutes to gain widespread adoption.

Coined by Peter Thiel in *Zero to One* (2014), this heuristic suggests that a new technology must be "at least ten times better" than substitutes at fulfilling some need in order to gain the necessary traction to dislodge incumbents.

Bitcoin offers a number of significant 10x advantages over transacting in the traditional financial system and over current methods of wealth preservation:

- accessibility (24/7/365)
- transaction finality
- storage, maintenance, and transportation costs
- censorship resistance
- independent auditability
- network redundancy

When combined with the optionality of using the lightning network for smaller-value and higher-frequency transactions, bitcoin breaks the model of assumed trade-offs for a monetary bearer instrument.

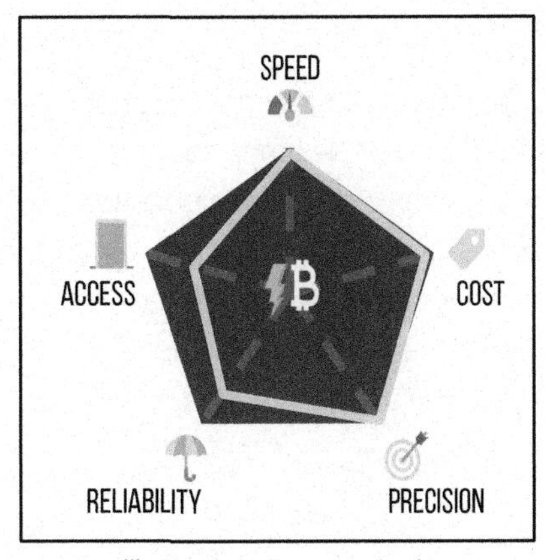

Illustrative purposes only

NETWORK EFFECTS

A phenomena whereby each additional user to a network adds disproportionately more value and utility.

Networks are how we transport cargo, people, and information from A→B. Methods that offer significant advantages (i.e., speed, cost, accessibility, reliability, precision) attract users, making the network more appealing to other users.

Digital networks that are superior across one or a combination of these dimensions can experience swift exponential growth due to network effects (a.k.a. Metcalfe's Law) since they can operate at a global scale, thus creating a single market.

"In network theory, the value of a system grows as approximately the square of the number of users of the system."

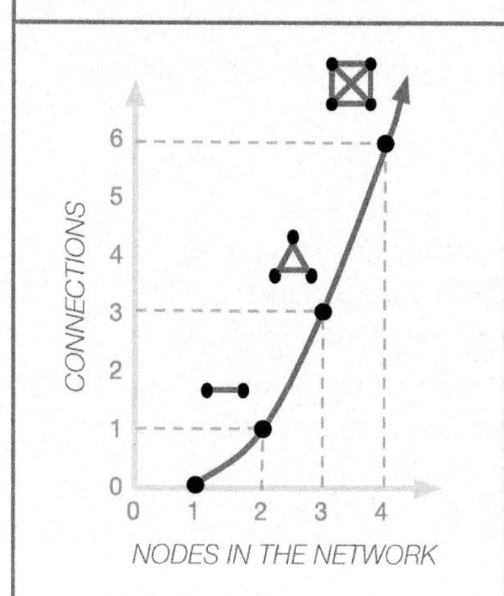

"I believe our evolutionary biology makes us hardwired to consistently underguess the power of modern, technological network effects, since nothing in our history resembles them."

-ROSS STEVENS

NETWORK EFFECTS

The bitcoin network currently consists of thousands of nodes (running specific software) and mining infrastructure (computing quintillions of hashes per second) worldwide.

Utilizing this network for transferring value offers the benefit of permissionless and censorship-resistant exchange with the assurance of final settlement in a unit that cannot be diluted. It is an astonishing improvement over the incumbent system.

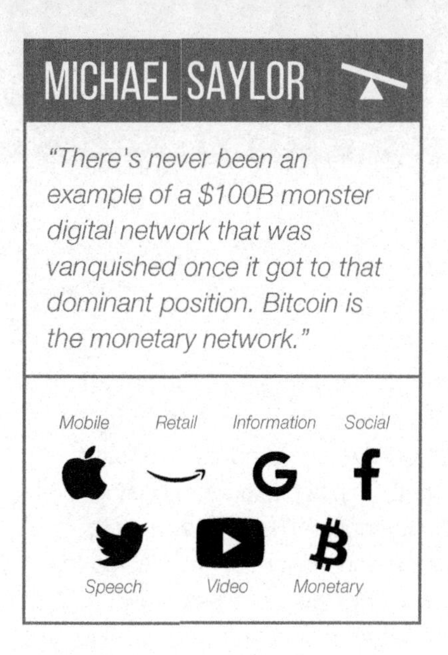

RELATED CONCEPT CHURN

The rate of user attrition, often expressed as a percentage.

Churn relates to the rate of user attrition. The concept is useful in establishing if a particular technology is on a growth trajectory (adoption > churn).

One way of measuring bitcoin adoption is observing the net migration of capital from the fiat system to bitcoin. Most notable is how it's often a permanent monetary upgrade, with remarkably few bitcoin users reverting back to fiat as their primary store of value.

Bitcoin's superior properties are difficult to unsee once conceptually grasped. It has re-ignited the monetary competition for storing and transacting value. This rate of net adoption has very real implications for an asset with a fixed terminal supply.

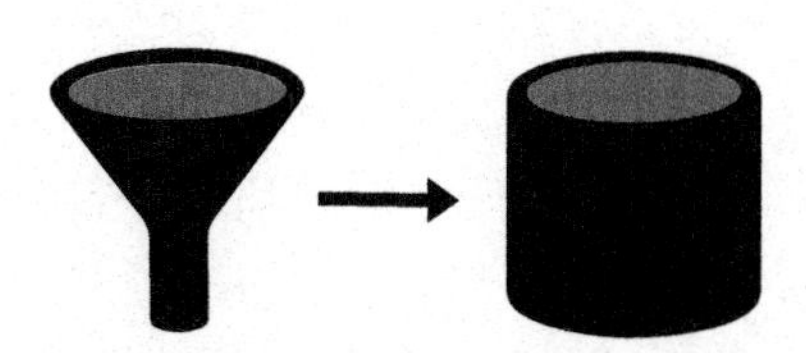

FRICTION

A force that opposes the relative movement of something.

Friction within a process or system increases the amount of energy required to overcome it. Think of traffic lights placed at a busy intersection. The objective is to increase friction for vehicles so that collisions become less likely. Another example is retail banking, which introduces (or fails to remove) friction to collect fees, increase control, and reduce fraud.

Moving value today via the traditional financial system is very much rooted in the Industrial Age. While most value may now be digital, the same delays, fragmentation, regulatory burdens, and censorship risks apply.

"Everything that moves has to move through something, including information."

-FARNAM STREET

Bitcoin was purpose-built as digitally-native money, enabling peer-to-peer transactions. Settlement friction is reduced by replacing third parties and permissions with transparent economic incentives (proof of work) and independent auditability. The result is a system with increased freedom of expression, lower transaction costs, increased final settlement speed, more innovation, and broader accessibility.

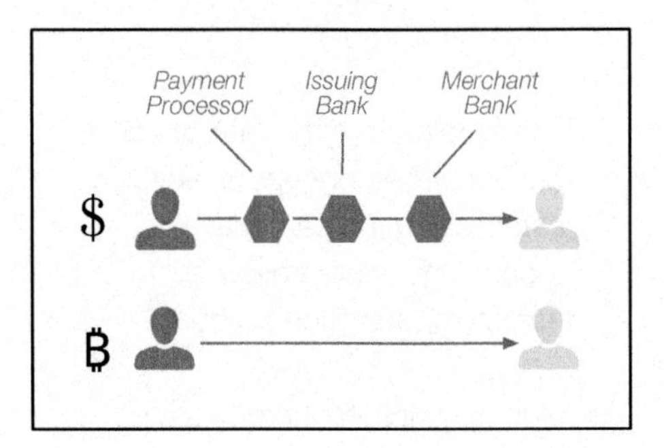

FRICTION

The bitcoin protocol turned money into pure information, enabling it to leverage the most appropriate communication methods and networks. As such, bitcoin will continue to benefit from the collective innovation in telecommunications and information technology.

"Before the browser, someone looks at TCP/IP and says, oh my God, this thing moves information from anywhere to anywhere real time and for free! It's going to change information forever. Well, hold on. Yes, but not now. Not for 20 years. Same thing with Bitcoin."

-WENCES CASARES

ROBERT BREEDLOVE

"In computer science, a protocol is a ruleset that governs the transmission of data. The internet is an integration of four successive layers of open-source protocols. In this context, Bitcoin can be considered the fifth layer of the internet protocol suite."

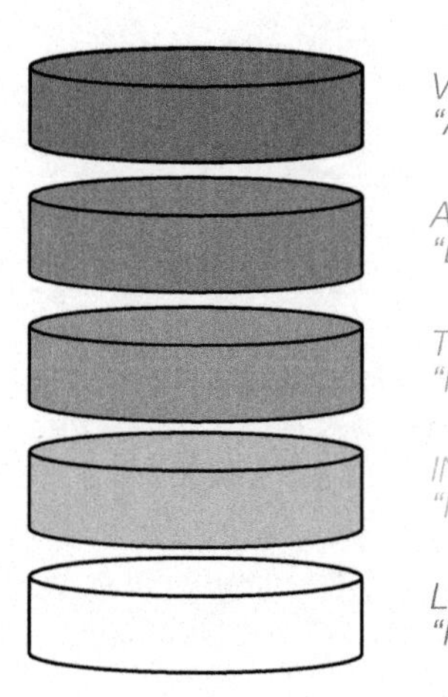

VALUE TRANSFER LAYER
"Allocates scarce resources across networks"

APPLICATIONLAYER
"Delivers software, files & applications"

TRANSPORT LAYER
"Persists communication across any given conversation"

INTERNET LAYER
"Routes data packets across networks"

LINK LAYER
"Puts data packets on the wire"

ACCELERATING RETURNS

The rate of technological change is exponential, resulting in ever-increasing innovation and disruption.

"An analysis of the history of technology shows that technological change is exponential...
So we won't experience 100 years of progress in the 21st century—it will be more like 20,000 years of progress (at today's rate)."

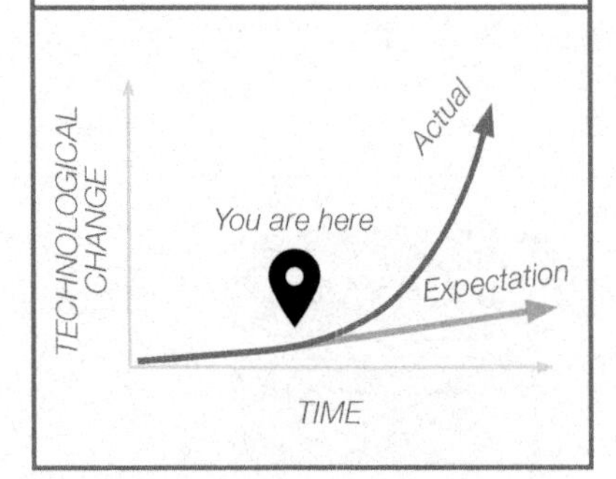

Technological change accelerates as humans continue to innovate on top of an ever-growing arsenal of existing technologies.

In just the previous two decades, we witnessed permanent behavioral shifts in the likes of retail shopping, entertainment, transportation, food services, and telecommunications. Money, as a technology, is not immune to such dramatic change.

The transition from one monetary order to another is not something many humans have lived to witness (see Relativity). The idea that it could happen within your lifetime seems implausible for this reason. Admitting to ourselves that we're poor predictors of technological change is the path to being open-minded enough to capitalize on these changes when they actually do occur.

"When it comes to history, we think in straight lines. [But] in order to think about the future correctly, you need to imagine things moving at a much faster rate than they're moving now."

-TIM URBAN

HIGHER ORDER EFFECTS

Actions have consequences.
And those consequences have consequences.

As a truly innovative monetary technology and network, bitcoin fundamentally and permanently alters our world. People will react to it, and there will be reactions to those reactions. As bitcoin grows, in terms of both adoption and value stored, so too will the magnitude of these reactions. Even then, many of the ripple effects that will result from bitcoin's creation remain unknown and inconceivable.

"Changing some aspect of a complex system always introduces Second-Order Effects, some of which may be antithetical to the original intent of the change. Elements..can be interrelated or dependent upon each other in millions of different ways."

-JOSH KAUFMAN

JEFF BOOTH

"Many people look at first-order effects, thinking in the short term. Conversely, not spending time considering the 2nd and 3rd order effects of actions—which leads them to put too much trust in a system that will ultimately fail."

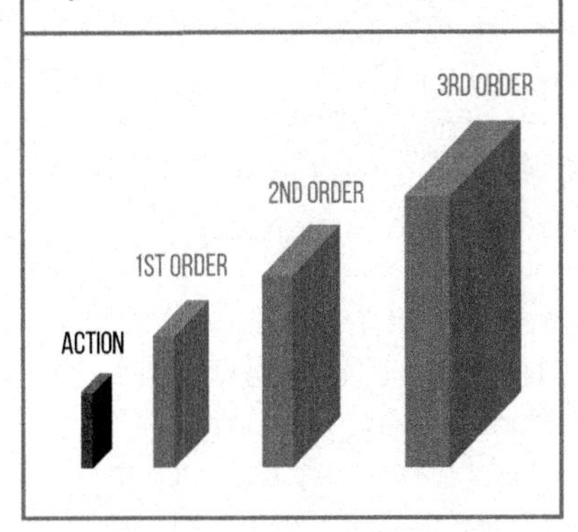

CREATIVE DESTRUCTION

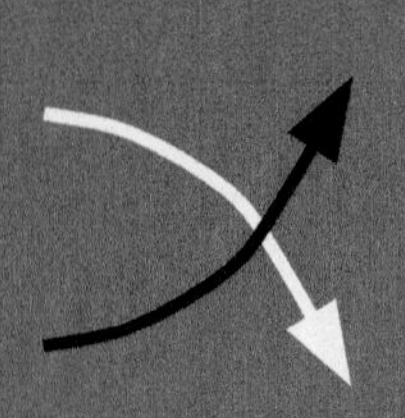

The cycle of entrepreneurs out-innovating and obsoleting incumbents under a free market.

Innovation is the process of combining existing tools and resources into something entirely new that is useful to society. It continually alters the incentives that govern our behavior, which disrupts incumbents and existing business models built around preserving the status quo.

Such advancements may come from any field (e.g., chemical engineering, freight transportation, I.T., etc.) and result in a fundamental step-function change in how society is organized.

Industries with monopolistic protections and artificially high barriers to entry eventually succumb to creative destruction at a more rapid pace due to prolonged underinvestment in research and development.

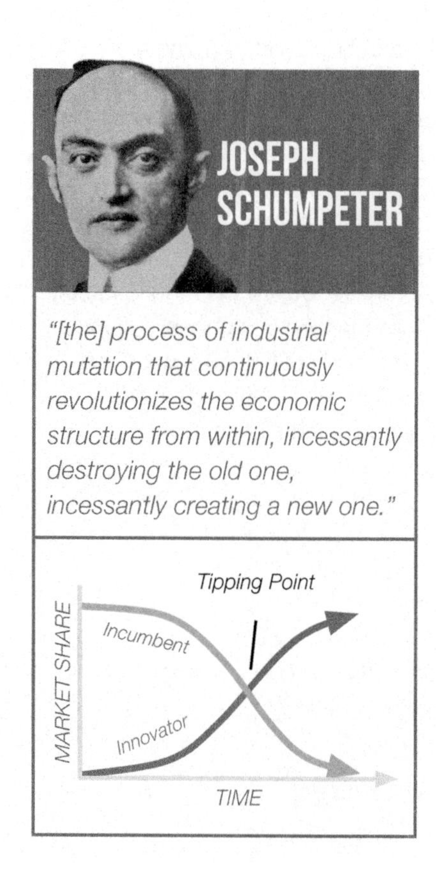

CREATIVE DESTRUCTION

Much like when the smartphone rendered a host of goods obsolete (e.g., newspapers, street directories, alarm clocks, etc.), bitcoin is dematerializing physical stores of value, brought about by the creation of a global and provably scarce digital bearer asset.

"You never change things by fighting the existing reality. To change something, build a new model that makes the existing model obsolete."

-BUCKMINSTER FULLER

When combined with the lightning network, bitcoin disrupts the system of central banking, sovereign currencies, and global settlement networks by offering an open parallel alternative void of such barriers and protections.

"If history's going to repeat itself, every time a digital successor has replaced an analog predecessor, [it] has dwarfed the analog predecessor by a tremendous amount."

-ERIC WEISS

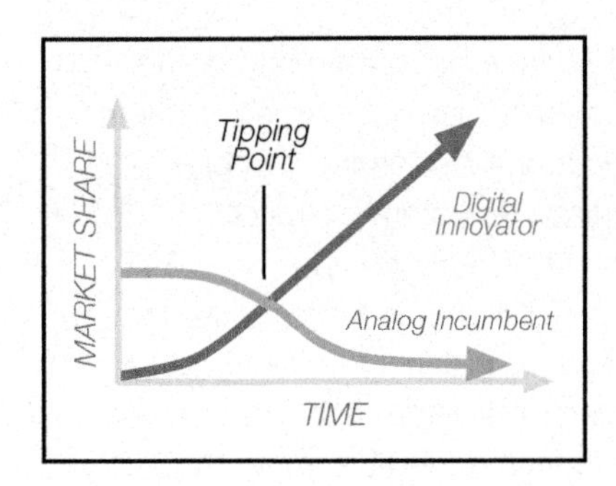

FEEDBACK LOOPS

When a system reacts to its environment, and the resultant output gets re-incorporated as an input, a feedback loop is created.

The fiat system is an attempt to centrally plan and manage what is a naturally emerging complex adaptive system by way of committee. Each time an 'undesirable' economic outcome occurs, this feedback is used to justify making adjustments, which are then added back into the system's design. Besides introducing unknowable personal biases and moral hazard into decisions, the process is entirely manual and subject to change.

Over time, these adjustments accumulate, causing spasms with increasing frequency and volatility. Like a car repeatedly steered in opposing directions; eventually, all control is lost.

Contrast this with a monetary system with no supply response to external economic feedback. Bitcoin simply functions as laid out in its public codebase, driving confidence in its continued operation.

Any and all feedback can only be reflected through changes in demand, driving multiple reinforcing feedback loops across variables such as hash rate, price, and adoption.

Δ Liquidity → Δ Volatility ↻

Δ Price → Δ Miner profitability →
Δ Competition → Δ Hashpower →
Δ Block time → Δ Difficulty adjustment ↻

FEEDBACK LOOPS

"Market-based economics is an engine designed to seek more efficient uses of capital by rewarding successful ventures and punishing the unsuccessful. A sound money system (like Bitcoin) improves this economic engine by tightening the feedback mechanism."

-BRANDON QUITTEM

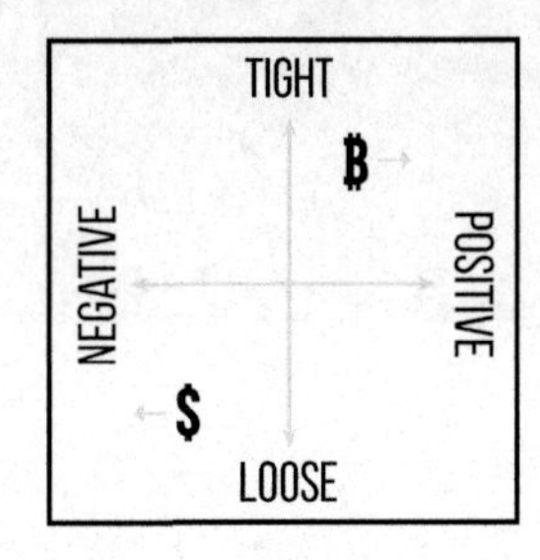

RELATED CONCEPT REFLEXIVITY

The circular relationship between market participants and sentiment, whereby it is hard to ascertain their respective impacts.

Market participants and the sentiment they hold can create a reflexive loop, where beliefs about the future may deviate significantly (positively or negatively) from economic fundamentals or historical averages.

Overreactions in markets are the result of several compounding factors:

- Participants have incomplete or inaccurate information
- Participants are subject to various biases
- Sentiment can be manipulated or influenced by various interests

Bitcoin's monetization journey has so far been marked by several boom and bust price cycles. At this early stage of maturity, bitcoin will likely continue to act reflexively for some time.

"The concept of reflexivity is crucial to understanding situations that have thinking participants. Reflexivity renders the participants' understanding imperfect and ensures that their actions will have unintended consequences."

RELATIVITY

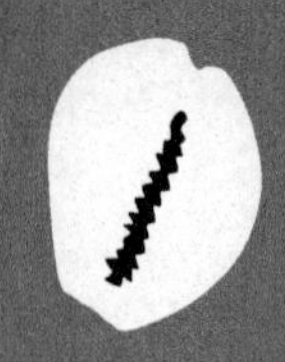

When you're a part of a system, it can be difficult to zoom out to gain perspective.

Relativity, in a general sense, implies the existence of something is dependent on some other entity for meaning or context.

This concept is helpful to consider in the context of money because it reminds us that multiple forms have previously existed and coexist today. Comparison enables us to determine which traits beget productivity and which invite debauchery.

We should also examine what the market has historically chosen as money and examine why. From seashells and salt to bronze and gold, primitive and metallic forms of money required some form of energy expenditure to collect or mine (see Thermodynamics) as a natural mechanism to protect against a flood in supply or unearned advantages.

Zooming out, it becomes apparent that we're living through a highly-abnormal monetary experiment impeding our ability to save, plan, and trade. In over 5,000 years of recorded monetary history, government-issued fiat currency has existed for roughly fifty.

VIJAY BOYAPATI

"The century between the gold standard and the Bitcoin standard- I call that the fiat interregnum. It's an anomaly of history, and it's not gonna last forever."

FIAT INTERREGNUM

GOLD STANDARD | BITCOIN STANDARD

THERMODYNAMICS: 1ST LAW

Energy cannot be created nor destroyed in isolatedsystems. It can only be transformed.

To explain the link between thermodynamics and bitcoin, let's start with understanding commodities. As a category of economic goods, commodities possess the property of fungibility, such that the market does not differentiate between who produced them.

All commodities (i.e., metals, agricultural, energy) require some form of energy conversion in their extraction or farming. Whether it be cattle consuming feed or an excavator combusting diesel, there is no substitute for this process. Bitcoin represents the world's first rivalrous digital commodity, anchoring issuance to energy expended (for computation) in the physical world.

"There is no shortcut to these computations, which is why the physics inherent in computation—the very physical process of flipping bits—is undeniably embedded in the information that is produced."

-GIGI

However, unlike other commodities, bitcoin's rate of issuance is predetermined and unaffected by fluctuations in the amount of energy employed in its production. This attribute is core to bitcoin's attractiveness as money. Issuance is meritocratic, while supply is known, verifiable, and enforceable.

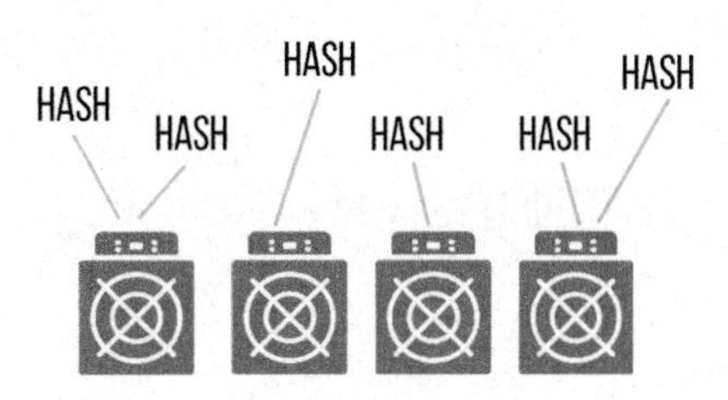

THERMODYNAMICS: 1ST LAW

Miners expend computational power (converting electricity into hashes and dissipating heat) in the search for a random number known as a nonce. When combined with transaction data, the resulting hash can permit miners to collect a reward if it meets current parameters.

This process increases the settlement assurances of already confirmed transactions by increasing the cost of altering history.

Incurring real-world resource costs incentivizes miners to submit valid work to the network, especially when validation is trivial. Attempting to include an invalid transaction in a proposed block would quickly be detected and rejected by nodes, but the computational work performed would have already been sacrificed.

"Consensus mechanisms that don't involve work... instead involve governance."

-LYN ALDEN

Bitcoin's proof of work consensus mechanism enables strangers to reach agreement without a third party, at regular intervals, as to which addresses contain bitcoin.

"Bitcoin is robust historical immutability by thermodynamic law. We only need one proof-of-work immutable ledger."

-ANDREAS ANTONOPOULOS

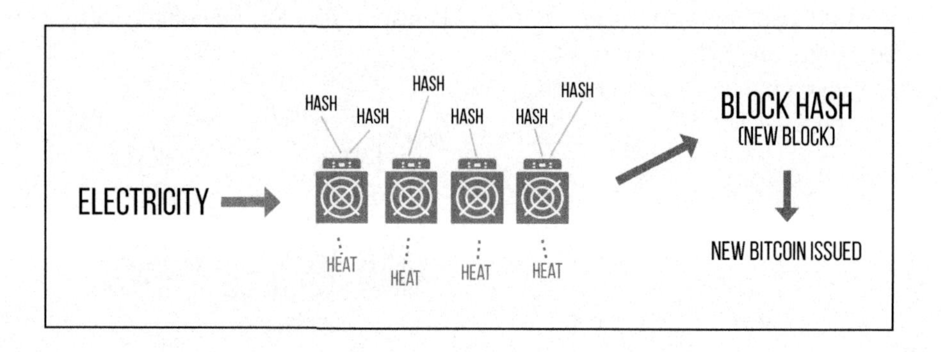

THERMODYNAMICS: 2ND LAW

The entropy of the universe always increases with time.

Thermodynamic entropy can be considered a measure of a system's disorder or randomness. Lower entropy, less randomness; higher entropy, more randomness.

The information about how the state of a system changes has to get observed, processed, and ultimately recorded somewhere.

Ordered systems in our world, such as a living human or the bitcoin blockchain, require constant input of energy such that useful work can be conducted to build and maintain that order. The by-product of this process is heat which can no longer do any useful work. Taken together, the ordered system and the energy consumed to maintain that order, plus the waste heat produced, ultimately increase the entropy of the universe as a whole consistent with the 2nd law.

But this is a one-way process. You can't combine heat with a human and get back the food they've already consumed. Similarly, with bitcoin's blockchain, the 2nd law ensures that the bitcoin clock can only run one way, and its past is increasingly locked in place by an ever-growing thermodynamic energy wall.

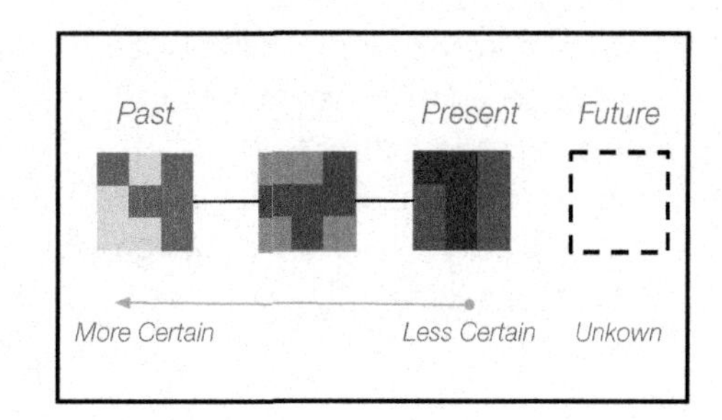

RELATED CONCEPT

ARROW OF TIME

Establishing the one-way direction of time by distinguishing past from present.

A chain is a series of links. bitcoin forms a tamper-evident sequence of its history by consistently linking the most recent block to the second most recent. The information contained in each block acts like cement drying in layers, becoming harder to impact with time.

Block production occurs at consistent intervals, regardless of computational power directed at the network, thanks to an ingenious mechanism that adjusts the difficulty level of finding a nonce to meet a target rate.

"The only thing that is truly ticking in the Bitcoin network is the global clock: a block clock, where every block is one unit of time."

-GIGI

The bitcoin protocol creates a consistent stream of information forged by energy conversion and locked by the 2nd law of thermodynamics. It provides us with the ability to distinguish the past from the present and independently establish the direction of time.

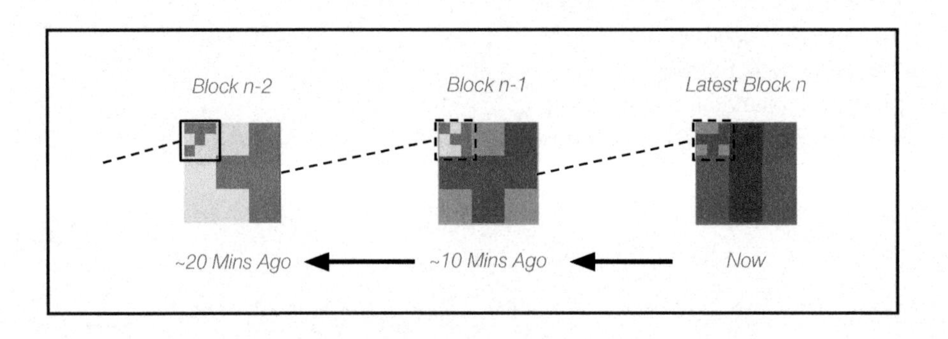

RELATED CONCEPT

INFORMATION THEORY

How digital information is communicated, stored, and quantified.

Information theory is the study of how digital information is communicated, stored, and quantified. At its core, this concept is concerned with the ability of the receiver to accurately reconstruct a message when faced with a noisy channel (caused by external interference).

In the case of a monetary network, redundancy of information storage is critical. Bitcoin's network of independent nodes enables retrieval, recreation, and validation of the entire chain with just one other peer. This attribute enables the network to function without a central authority and increases the odds of network survivability.

"The fundamental problem of communication is that of reproducing at one point, either exactly or approximately, a message selected at another point."

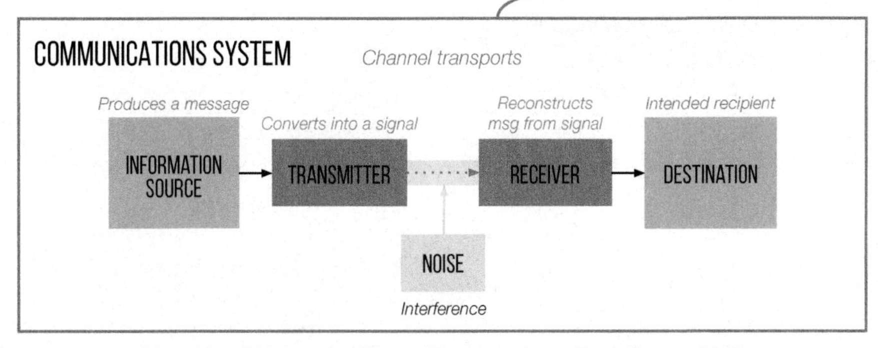

Adapted from A Mathematical Theory of Communication by Claude Shannon (1949).

MOORE'S LAW

The observation that the number of transistors on a computer chip doubles approximately every two years.

Technology deflation is a beautiful thing. It enables us to reap the compounding benefits of innovation. Whether that means reducing the inputs required in a process or achieving increased performance from the same inputs.

The effect of microprocessors on every aspect of modern life is astonishing. They've radically altered how we behave and communicate and are gradually shifting how society has been structured since the Industrial Age.

Moore's Law helps explain the exponential growth we've witnessed in computational power due to increasing density and falling costs over the last 50 years.

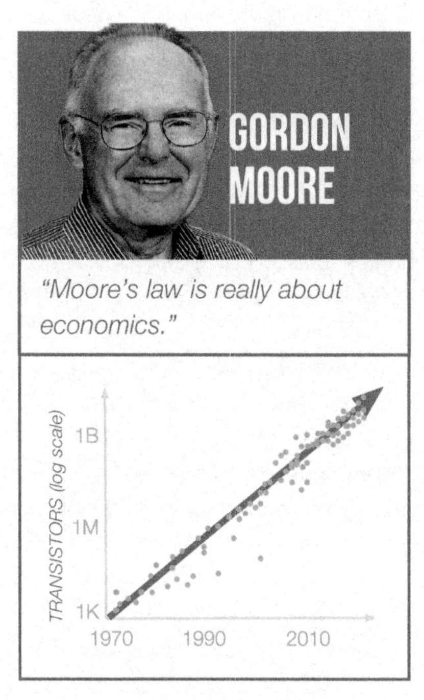

"The universal deployment of these increasingly powerful microprocessors... has affected every sector of manufacturing, transportation, services, and communication... accompanied by steadily declining costs and improving reliability."

-VACLAV SMIL

MOORE'S LAW

The bitcoin network benefits from this phenomenon as network nodes continue to proliferate around the world. If any monetary network is to be capable of resisting jurisdiction-specific attacks, it must achieve a certain threshold of decentralization among nodes that makes it infeasible to shut down.

Therefore, the ability to operate a node and independently verify transactions must be within reach for a sufficiently large number of people. The availability and the costs of necessary hardware are key factors in this.

"[microprocessors] have incubated a whole range of technologies that enhance the capacity of small groups and even individuals to function independently of central authority."

-DAVIDSON & REES-MOGG

Unlike miners, validating nodes don't require top-of-the-line hardware or varying degrees of computational power. Additionally, the linear growth of the blockchain (in terms of memory) means that future storage needs are predictable and negligible.

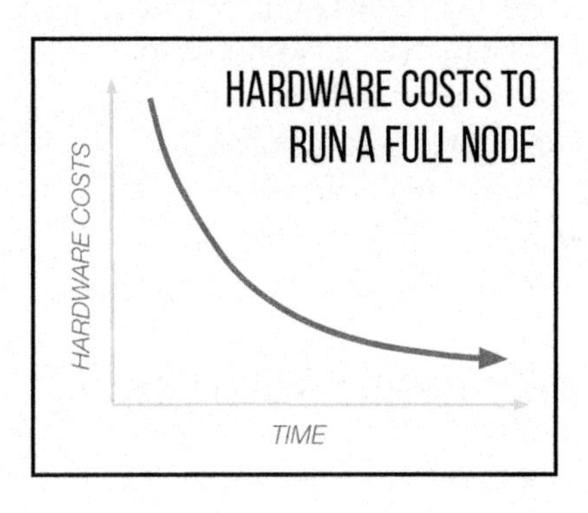

ANTIFRAGILITY

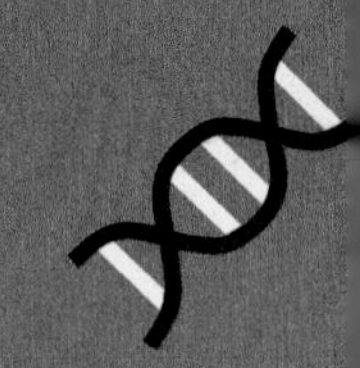

A property of certain things that actively gain from volatility and unpredictability by using rapid feedback loops to evolve.

The bitcoin network is not just difficult to kill, it actively becomes more resilient with each attempt (like muscle tissue repairing stronger after a strenuous workout). This is due to its peer-to-peer network architecture.

No single point of failure exists, as every full node possesses a valid history of the blockchain and all nodes exist on equal footing in the eyes of the protocol.

"There are no special bitcoin nodes; all nodes are the same."

-ANDREAS ANTONOPOULOS

Over time, the bitcoin network has grown in size (# of reachable nodes) and become increasingly decentralized as a result. It is now capable of withstanding and hardening from nation-state-level attacks.

"Given the unattainability of perfect robustness, we need a mechanism by which the system regenerates itself continuously by using, rather than suffering from, random events, unpredictable shocks, stressors, and volatility."

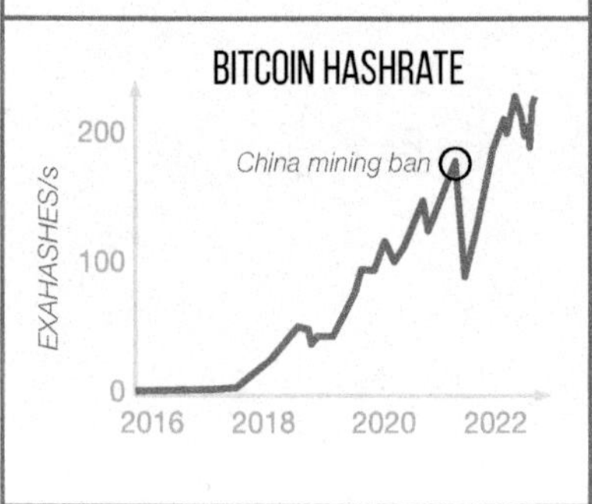

ANTIFRAGILITY

"When something is a decentralized, organic creature that is rapidly evolving and adapting, it becomes excessively antifragile because every time you kill it or an element of it, the elements you don't kill get that much stronger."

-MICHAEL SAYLOR

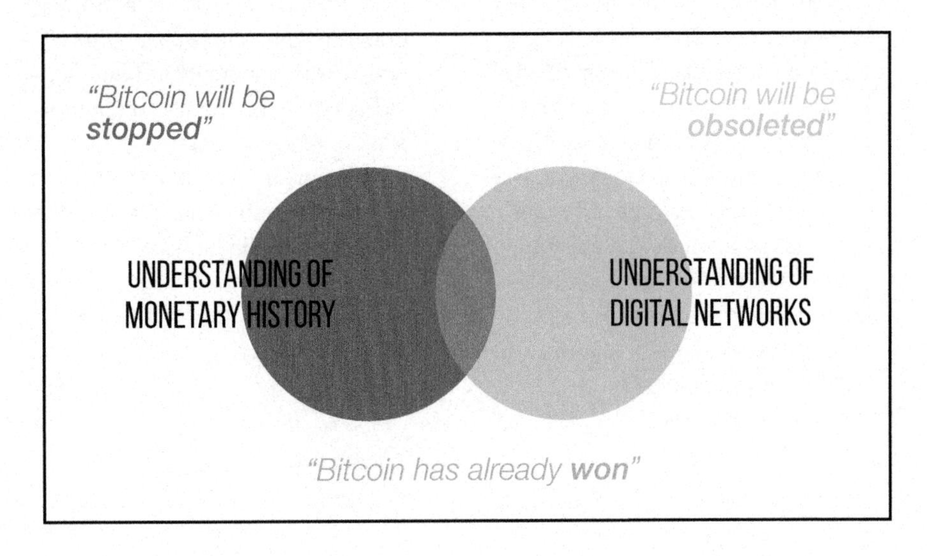

GALL'S LAW

Incremental improvements made to a functional system is superior to building a complex system from scratch.

Taken from John Gall's book Systemantics: How Systems Really Work and How They Fail (1977), this heuristic explains the success behind the systems we take for granted today, which evolved from simple yet reliable foundations. The same attitude was (and continues to be) taken towards developing the bitcoin protocol. A steadfast foundation grows long-term confidence for investments of time, capital, and technology infrastructure adoption.

"Creeping featurism is the tendency to add to the number of features that a device can do, often extending the number beyond all reason.. But each new set of features adds immeasurably to the size and complexity of the system."

-DONALD NORMAN

Complex systems are less able to respond with flexibility to entropy as one must take into account how any minor change will impact many individual components. In contrast, simple, functional systems may enable innovation (through iteration) as an extension, without risk to the underlying foundation.

"Bitcoin is too important to follow the Silicon Valley mantra of move fast and break things. Instead, it's move slowly and don't break anything. If a global financial system is to be built on a decentralized monetary system, the foundation must be protected at all cost."

-PARKER LEWIS

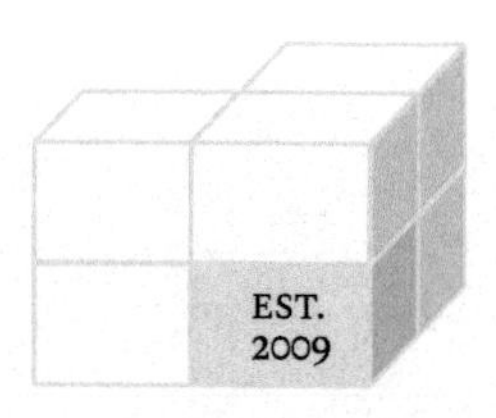

RELATED CONCEPT

ATTACK SURFACE

The sum of all potential vulnerabilities from all potential access points.

Imagine a fortress that must defend its walls from oncoming attacks. Minimizing the length of the perimeter that needs to be secured becomes a crucial design element, as square is easier to defend than a rectangle.

A key factor in bitcoin's resilience is the simplicity of the core protocol coupled with the high degree of scrutiny it receives as an open-source project.

"Cramming all the features of lightning, Liquid, DLCs, RGB, and so on, into the mainchain.. is just an obviously bad idea. It would introduce unknowable attack vectors and hence holistic fragility."

-ALLEN FARRINGTON & BIG AL

Enabling permissionless experimentation on top of bitcoin without threatening the foundation is fundamental to scaling and innovation in general.

SATOSHI NAKAMOTO

"Being open source means anyone can independently review the code. If it was closed source, nobody could verify the security."

```
CAmount GetBlockSubsidy(int nHeight,
const Consensus::Params&
consensusParams)
{
    int halvings = nHeight /
consensusParams.nSubsidyHalvingInterval;
    // Force block reward to zero when
right shift is undefined.
    if (halvings >= 64)
        return 0;

    CAmount nSubsidy = 50 * COIN;
    // Subsidy is cut in half every
210,000 blocks which will occur
approximately every 4 years.
    nSubsidy >>= halvings;
    return nSubsidy;
}
```

CATALYSTS

Kick-starts a reaction but isn't itself a reactant.

In chemistry, a catalyst modifies the reaction rate between a substance and reactants without being impacted. In a broader sense, a catalyst precipitates some kind of change when introduced into an environment.

Satoshi Nakamoto devised an ingenious method to prevent duplicating digital cash (double-spending) without reliance on an intermediary. This solution was codified in the bitcoin protocol and released into the wild.

While it is not certain, a message left by Satoshi in the genesis block could indicate that the bailouts received by financial institutions post-2008 were a catalyst for bitcoin.

"Bitcoin may also represent the biggest catalyst the world has ever known for developing abundant, clean, cheap energy. And, therefore, one of biggest catalysts in the world for human flourishing."

-ROSS STEVENS

As digitally-native sound money, accessible to all, bitcoin has become a catalyst. By introducing a new choice, bitcoin compels people to compare the attributes of competing monetary goods (e.g., scarcity, durability, portability, etc.).

Many of the shifts that bitcoin will catalyze are unknowable, but if current developments are anything to go by, they will be nothing short of tremendous.

3 JAN 2009

THE TIMES

CHANCELLOR ON BRINK OF SECOND BAILOUT FOR BANKS

PART III: Psychology

PRISONER'S DILEMMA

Using math to determine if it's better to cooperate or compete in multiplayer games.

Decisions involving multiple parties, where coordination offers the greatest benefit, must consider the preferences of others. The prisoner's dilemma is an exercise that helps model the range of outcomes and the optimal course of action in such a situation.

At an international level, bitcoin, as a competitor to other forms of money, forces sovereign nations into pursuing a strategy, whether proactively (ban) or passively (allow).

As several countries have now demonstrated that banning bitcoin is unenforceable, the optimal strategy becomes to accept and regulate or watch capital and talent migrate to countries that impose less friction. To take this logic one step further, governments must now consider whether to hold bitcoin as part of their reserves as a hedge.

If bitcoin does become the dominant digital global money, it will have done so by severely demonetizing all other forms of money and sovereign bonds.

CHRIS KULPER & JACK NEUREUTER

"If bitcoin adoption increases, the countries that secure some bitcoin today will be better off competitively than their peers. Therefore, even if other countries do not believe in the investment thesis.., they will be forced to acquire some as a form of insurance."

	Country B *Bans*	**Country B** *Allows*
Country A *Bans*	↑ Ban fails Adoption	Capital flows A → B
Country A *Allows*	Capital flows B → A	↑ Trade & consumer choice

Source: Parker Lewis, "Bitcoin Cannot Be Banned"

PRISONER'S DILEMMA

"The process of monetization is game-theoretic; every market participant attempts to anticipate the aggregate demand of other participants and thereby the future monetary premium."

-VIJAY BOYAPATI

RELATED CONCEPT

JURISDICTIONAL ARBITRAGE

Taking advantage of discrepancies between competing legal jurisdictions.

The option to emigrate to where one has the best relative circumstances (i.e., lower cost of living, higher quality of life, higher salary, etc.) is a real threat to the future tax revenue of nation-states. In an era where the highly skilled are increasingly mobile and coveted by multiple jurisdictions, leverage is returned to the skilled.

ADAM FERGUSSON

"Evasion of taxation, fear of socialisation, and inflation have combined to drive capital out of countries with a depreciated currency into countries where the currency is sound or at a premium."

WHEN MONEY DIES

SOCIAL PROOF

In uncertain situations, we look to those we deem more knowledgeable or competent for guidance on how best to think or act.

Bitcoin has received its fair share of fear, uncertainty, and doubt due to its novelty and lack of familiar parallels. This has left much of the general public misinformed and skeptical. However, over time, bitcoin has become more socially acceptable as a growing chorus of reputable individuals and institutions signal their endorsement of the technology.

Radically new things will always be met with skepticism and caution by the general public. Social proof performs the valuable task of efficiently dispelling fear, uncertainty, and doubt at scale.

Capital allocators face genuine career risk for betting on new technologies too early in their adoption curve. But eventually, the opportunity cost becomes too great to continue to ignore a permanent shift in consumer behavior.

"Paul Tudor Jones validates it for other hedge fund managers, hedge fund managers validate it for sovereign-wealth funds, sovereign-wealth funds will validate it for central banks."

-NAVAL RAVIKANT

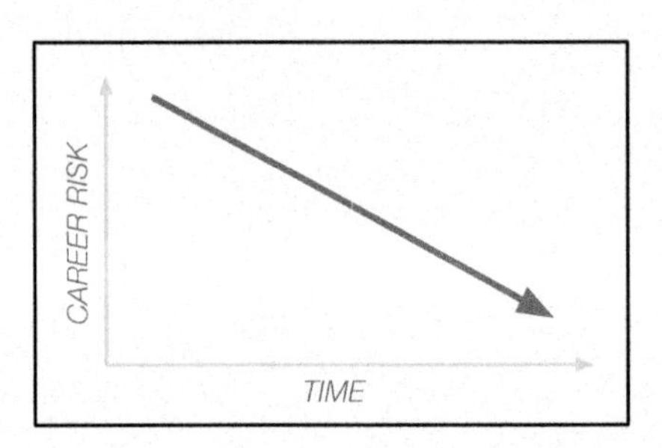

RELATED CONCEPT

MIMETIC THEORY

In uncertain situations, we look to those we deem more knowledgeable or competent for guidance on how best to think or act.

Not everybody using the dollar today understands why it's the vehicle of choice for savings and transactions. The same will be true for bitcoin at saturation. Some people will consciously choose bitcoin because it's the hardest money. Others will simply imitate this preference. Both will contribute to a positive feedback loop.

"Models are people or things that show us what is worth wanting. It is models—not our 'objective' analysis or central nervous system—that shape our desires. With these models, people engage in a secret and sophisticated form of imitation that Girard termed mimesis, from the Greek word mimeisthai (to imitate)."

-LUKE BURGIS

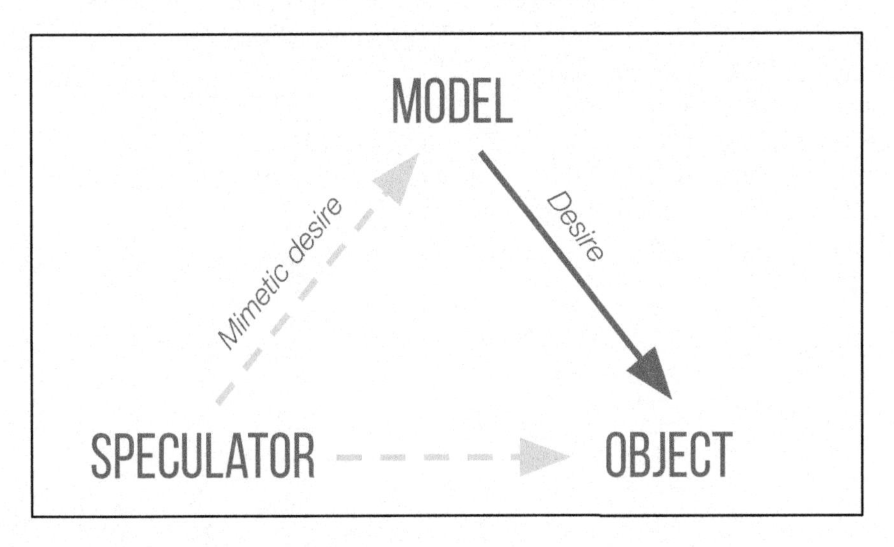

FIRST CONCLUSION BIAS

The tendency to accept the first answer offered, regardless of correctness, shutting out any further inquiry or debate.

Your initial conclusions about new technologies are often incorrect or incomplete, but you're still likely to defend them. This is ultimately disadvantageous to you.

"The mind works a bit like a sperm and egg: the first idea gets in and then the mind shuts... leads us to accept many erroneous results."

-CHARLIE MUNGER

Everyone initially misunderstands bitcoin to some degree simply because there is nothing comparable that exists. Digital scarcity is an entirely new concept with many yet unknown implications that people must wrap their heads around.

Our continued survival is largely a product of our ability to quickly identify and assess risk. So while you may shake your head in frustration at those who disregard or disparage bitcoin as a Ponzi scheme, cult or, failed experiment, remember that it's just an ingrained reactionary mechanism to the unfamiliar. A neutral curiosity and the testing of assumptions is required in order to be truly secure in your conclusions.

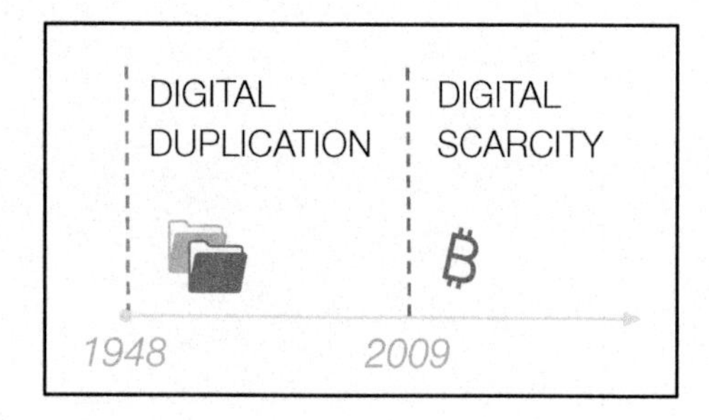

CIRCLE OF COMPETENCE

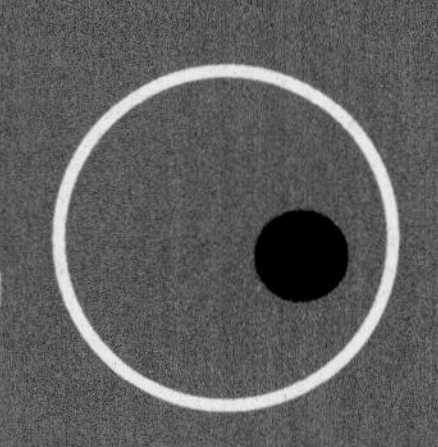

Understanding where your knowledge is lacking will illuminate where you're vulnerable.

We all have unique experiences and knowledge that give us narrow areas of expertise. But most of the time, we must operate outside them, making sense as best we can. This is harmless in situations of minor consequence, but it can become problematic when the stakes are high.

The ability to clearly define the boundaries of one's intellectual competency, and avoid the lure of overconfidence, reduces the chances of mistakes and failures. In most scenarios, a beginner's mindset will serve us best.

Bitcoin is conceptually challenging to understand because it requires an interdisciplinary approach spanning several seemingly unrelated but overlapping fields (e.g., thermodynamics, hardware, monetary history, cryptography, etc.).

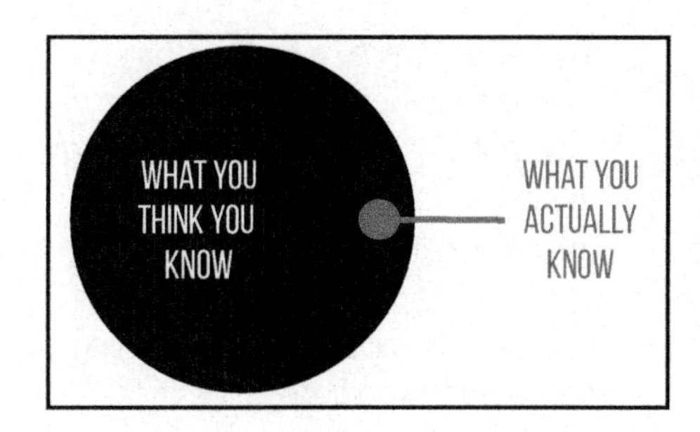

"It is really important to stay within your circle of competence. If you are not sure what the boundaries of that circle are for you, then you do not have real mastery of your field."

-CHARLIE MUNGER

"Believe me, man is capable of somehow creating more bitcoin... They tell you there are rules and they can't do it. Don't believe them. When there is enough incentive, bad things will happen."

-CHARLIE MUNGER

CIRCLE OF COMPETENCE

Assessing it solely through a narrow lens of expertise means failing to see the wider system. Fortunately, your circle of competence is not some static thing, and you can shape it over time.

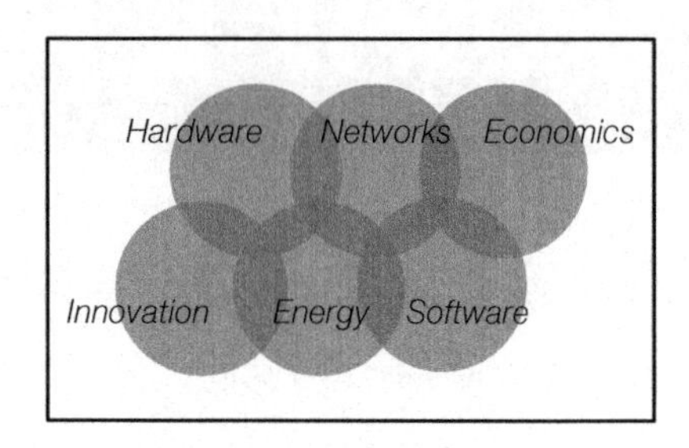

RELATED CONCEPT DUNNING-KRUGER EFFECT

Overestimating your knowledge in a specific area leads to erroneous decisions.

This related bias describes the tendency to hold overly favorable views of one's abilities while lacking the self-awareness to recognize it (metacognition).

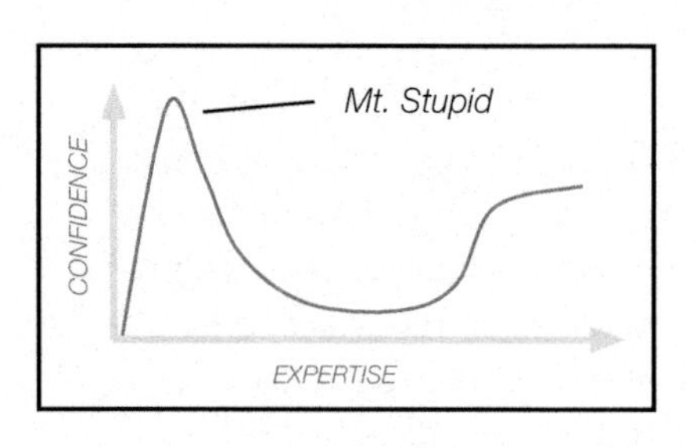

In their 1999 paper, David Dunning and Justin Kruger describe the 'dual burden' of being incapable of recognizing one's social and intellectual shortcomings while simultaneously making poor decisions based on the false conclusions reached.

"Bitcoin appears superficially simple, which is good for adoption and interest... but... the design gets more counter-intuitive as you get into the details."

-ADAM BACK

CATEGORY ERROR

Assuming an individual property of something is representative of its whole, leading to misattribution.

Critics regularly run afoul by assessing bitcoin against their mistaken beliefs about what it is. Most commonly, comparing bitcoin's short-term volatility to the U.S. dollar when it's held primarily as a long-term savings vehicle or decrying bitcoin as an investment because it pays no dividend (despite appreciating by >100% per year on average over the last decade).

Everyone has an opinion on how to classify bitcoin, but in reality, bitcoin defies absolute categorization due to its many facets in a constantly evolving environment.

MARTY BENT

"Bitcoin is not a stock, nor is it a startup or an investment fund... this is a completely different animal than the other types of assets that people are trying to compare it to. You need to view it through a different lens."

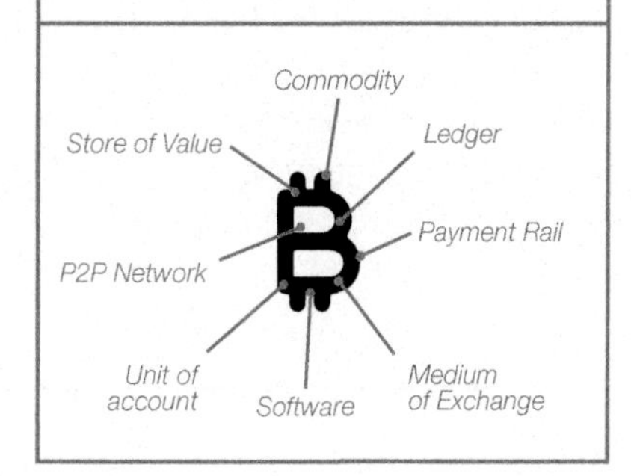

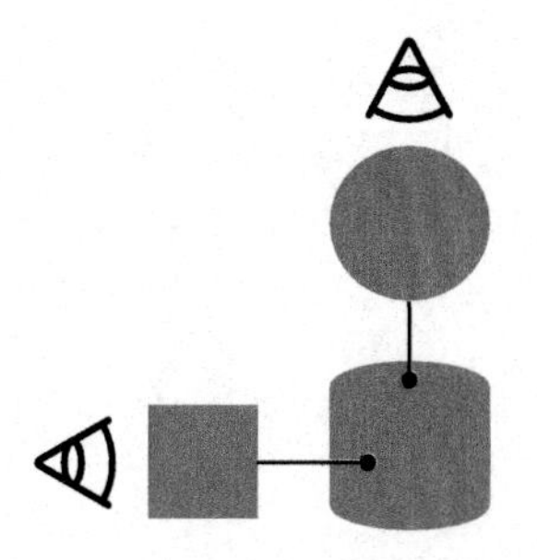

GARTNER HYPE CYCLE

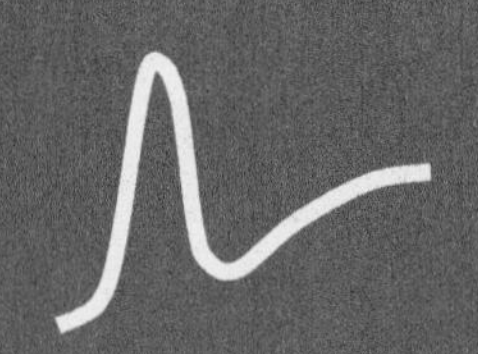

A methodology for ascertaining the maturity and adoption of new technologies and applications.

Technologies get adopted in waves. It's a constant game of cat and mouse between the maturity of a technology and people's expectations.

The Gartner Hype Cycle explains the evolving phases of public perception around emerging technologies. However, it is rarely a one-time journey for genuine breakthroughs but a series of hype cycles, each increasing in magnitude (see Intransigent Minority: innovation diffusion theory).

As we witness these cyclical explosions in users, capital, developers, and products, nothing can replace the advantage of long-term conviction, developed through genuine curiosity and first-hand experimentation.

"The earliest buyers in a Gartner hype cycle typically have a strong conviction about the transformative nature of the technology they are investing in."

-VIJAY BOYAPATI

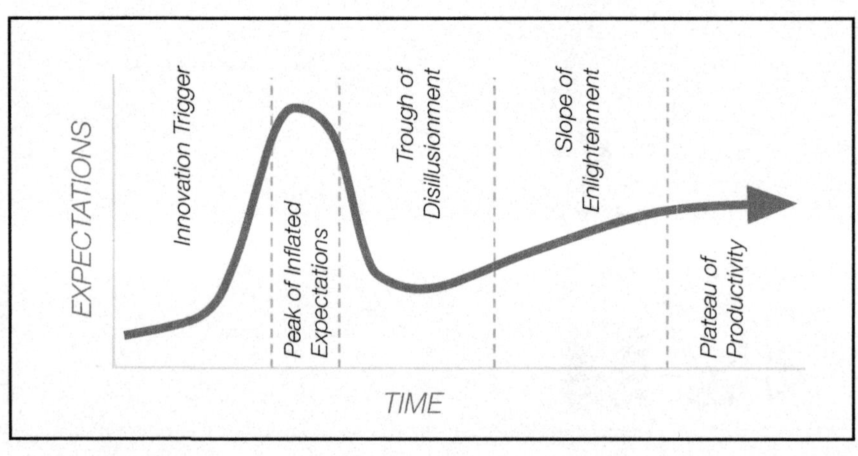

RELATED CONCEPT

AMARA'S LAW

The mismatch of time horizons between our expectations for new technologies and their actual impact.

We naturally get excited about new technologies that have the potential to improve our standard of living or enable us to do the previously impossible. This results in our expectations getting ahead of reality. New technologies take time to develop, stabilize and become intuitive enough for widespread adoption (something necessary for network effects to emerge).

Amara's Law differs from Gartner's Hype Cycle in that it highlights how we tend to think in linear terms when the process of commercializing innovation is anything but!

"Forecasting technological change is almost impossibly hard and nobody — yes, nobody — is an expert at it. The only sensible course is to be wary of the initial hype but wary too of the later scepticism."

-MATT RIDLEY

"We tend to overestimate the effect of a technology in the short run and underestimate the effect in the long run."

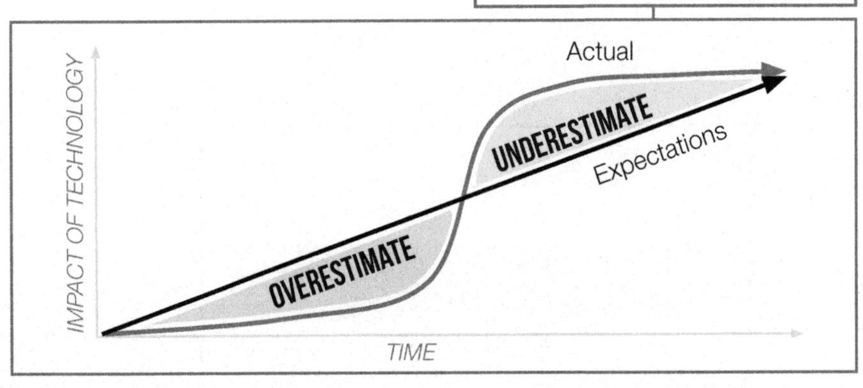

INTRANSIGENT MINORITY

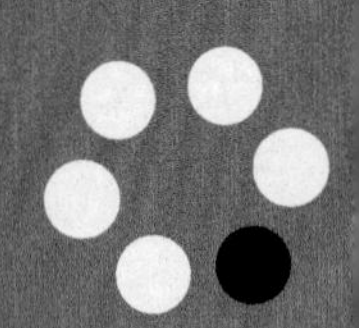

When a few individuals shape the preferences of the majority by their unwillingness to submit to the default option.

Popularized by Nassim Taleb in his 2018 book, Skin In The Game, this concept highlights the speed at which society-wide change can occur from seemingly small beginnings.

Bitcoin users are slowly forcing their preferences on the market through an unwillingness to use fiat currency as their denominator in economic calculations (due to its unpredictability in supply).

As a result, products and services have been built to accommodate this growing audience, further proliferating adoption. This is ultimately how all innovations are adopted (i.e., diffusion of innovation theory).

"If a very small minority converges on the belief that bitcoin has superior monetary properties and will not accept your form of digital (or traditional) currency as money, while less convicted market participants accept both bitcoin and other currencies, the intolerant minority wins."

-PARKER LEWIS

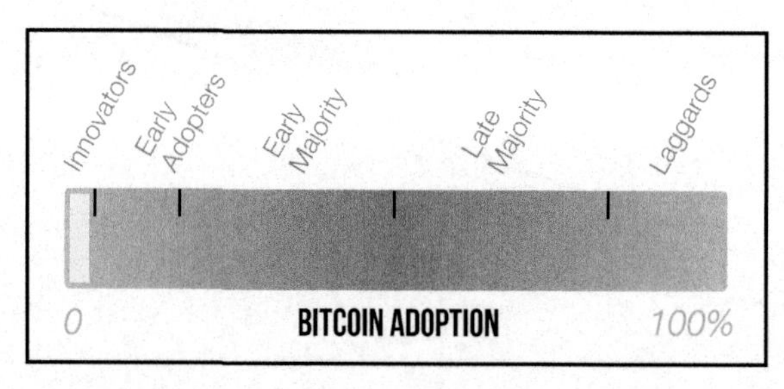

INEQUIVALENCE THEOREM

When economic conditions become excessively burdensome, individuals with the capacity will permanently exit a jurisdiction.

Expanding on economist David Ricardo's Equivalence Theorem, Davidson and Rees-Mogg propose that as sovereign nations continue to issue debt at an accelerating rate, those with the means will seek to emigrate in an effort to avoid anticipated societal decline and increased rates of taxation required to pay it off.

"Governments that overburdened their taxpayers... ended up on the dust-heap of history."

-NICK SZABO

JAMES DALE DAVIDSON & WILLIAM REES-MOGG

"In the Information Age.. the rational person will not respond to the prospect of higher taxes to fund deficits.. Sovereign individuals and other rational people will flee jurisdictions with large unfunded liabilities."

Bitcoin makes capital dilution-proof, truly portable, and extraordinarily difficult to confiscate, giving the individual leverage over extractive authoritarian and socialist regimes.

"IF THERE IS AN ESCAPE, THAT ESCAPE WILL BE USED."

-CHRISTINE LAGARDE

GELL-MANN AMNESIA EFFECT

Observing errors in the reporting of a topic, yet trusting the same source in areas where you are less knowledgeable.

It is understandably frustrating when a journalistic publication produces inaccurate reporting on a topic in which you have expertise. But we should use this signal as a warning for the general accuracy level in all other reporting areas.

Bitcoin is complex on the first pass, making for low-hanging fruit in sensational journalism. But, as an open-source communications tool, attempts to make predictions or attach moralistic labels should raise red flags.

MICHAEL CRICHTON

You open the newspaper to an article on some subject you know well..and see the journalist has absolutely no understanding of either the facts or the issues.., and read as if the rest of the newspaper was somehow more accurate."

Newsweek

Bitcoin Mining on Track to Consume All of the World's Energy by 2020

11 DEC. 2017

"The press generally gets things wrong that are:

- *too new*
- *too technical*
- *too multidisciplinary*
- *hurt too many interests*
- *create too much interest*
- *things... in general."*

-GIACOMO ZUCCO

LINDY EFFECT

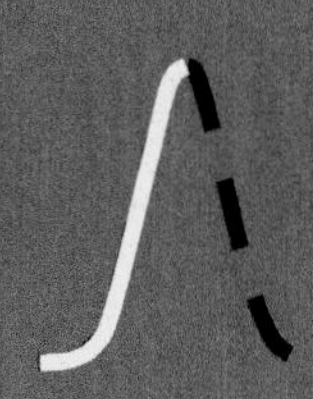

The theory that the lifespan of non-perishable things is proportional to their current age.

Bitcoin is now more than a decade mature. While this is minuscule in monetary history, it's significant for a digital network and unprecedented for a digital, non-sovereign monetary network.

The Lindy Effect (a.k.a Lindy's Law) helps us consider the likelihood of bitcoin's continued existence. As blocks continue to be produced and transactions settled, confidence grows in the network's ongoing immutability. This becomes a self-reinforcing cycle, and the time horizon by which people store wealth in bitcoin lengthens.

"Every day that goes by and Bitcoin hasn't collapsed due to legal or technical problems, that brings new information to the market. It increases the chance of Bitcoin's eventual success and justifies a higher price."

-HAL FINNEY

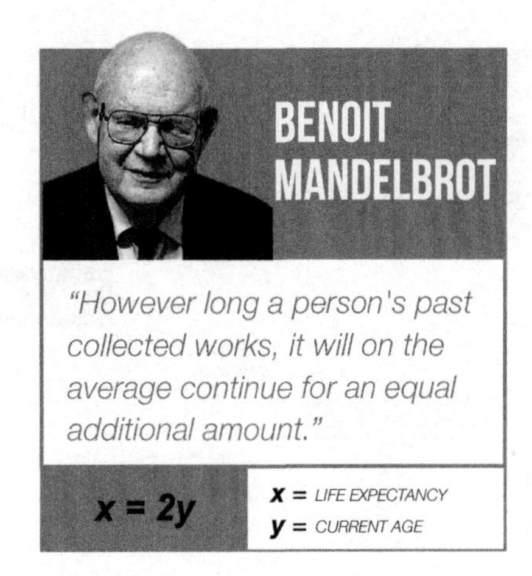

LINDY EFFECT

"Innovation..breaks open the Lindy effect. Only a paradigm shift justifies the time and energy expenditure needed to make the long and burdensome transition from one protocol to another.

Lindy Cycles of succeeding technologies can temporarily overlap during the adoption phase of the next generation technology."

-WILLEM VAN DEN BERGH

DAYS SINCE THE
BITCOIN NETWORK
HAS BEEN DOWN:
3,643
As of 4 March 2023

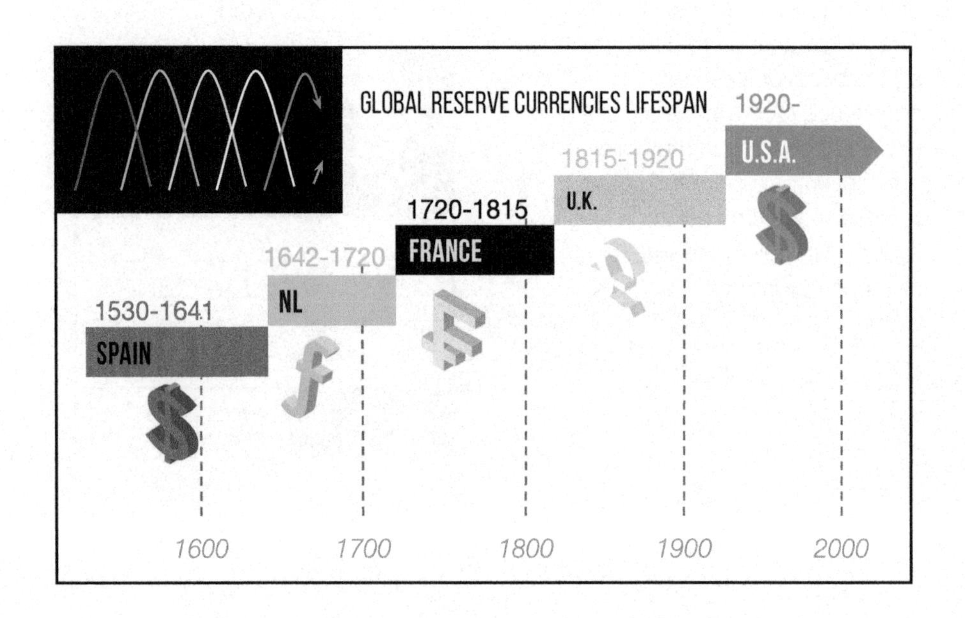

EMERGENCE

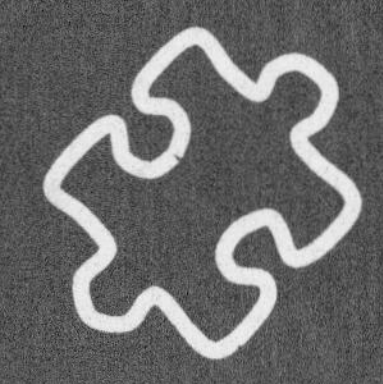

When novel dynamic structures arise from the interaction of individual components and becomes self-regulating.

While the individual parts laid out in the bitcoin whitepaper work in concert, largely as described, the higher-order effects and incentivized behavior are wholly unpredictable.

"Monetary status is a spontaneously emergent product of human action..not something that is conferred through academic debate, rational planning, or government mandate."

-SAIFEDEAN AMMOUS

From hash functions and Merkle trees to a proof of work consensus mechanism, bitcoin harnesses many tools and technologies that spur economic incentives, making it increasingly formidable money over time.

JAMESON LOPP

"Bitcoin didn't appear out of thin air—it is the result of decades of work. Many digital currency projects failed before it succeeded. Understanding how we got here will help you understand where we're going."

EMERGENCE

The monetization of bitcoin is unlikely to progress in an orderly fashion. Bitcoin does not exist in a vacuum, and there are many variables to consider. As knowledge disseminates unevenly, multiple users will be concurrently at different points on the path.

"Bitcoin is currently transitioning from the first stage of monetization to the second stage... No one alive has seen the real-time monetization of a good (as is taking place with Bitcoin), so there is precious little experience regarding the path this monetization will take."

-VIJAY BOYAPATI

COLLECTIBLE → STORE OF VALUE → MEDIUM OF EXCHANGE → UNIT OF ACCOUNT

STREISAND EFFECT

Attempting to hide, remove, or censor something has the unintended consequence of publicizing it more widely.

In 2003, singer Barbra Streisand sought to suppress an aerial photo containing her Malibu residence from a public webpage. A lawsuit against the photographer garnered significant publicity and resulted in over 400,000 additional image views. The image had previously been downloaded just six times.

We regularly witness the Streisand effect each time a government attempts to ban, dissuade use, or smear bitcoin. As a truly decentralized network, banning bitcoin only reveals the limits of government power.

In times of accelerating currency debasement, governments that play up bitcoin's perceived shortcomings simply elicit greater skepticism for the existing fiat system. Fortunately, we now have a universal instrument, immune to government threat or action that acts as a mirror for the real-time market value of fiat currencies.

"Bitcoin has been banned many times in many geographies, and yet today adoption is outpacing internet adoption."

-ALYSE KILLEEN

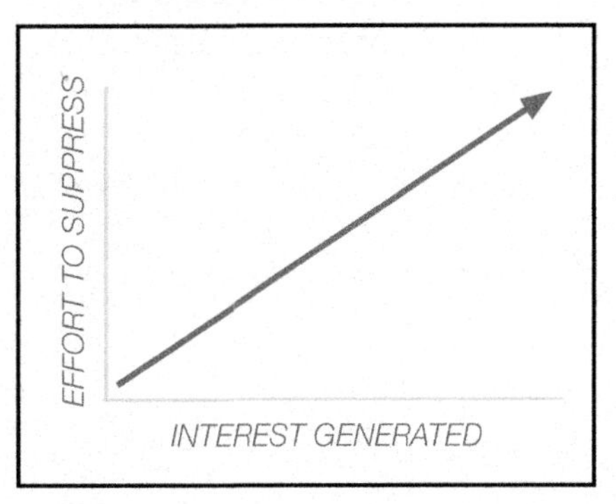

MORAL HAZARD

A party with a duty to serve the interests of others but is incentivized to prioritize its own interests.

Individuals or institutions that aren't forced to face the full consequences of their decisions will inevitably see their appetite for risk increase beyond prudence.

"Capitalism without bankruptcy is like Christianity without hell."

-FRANK BORMAN

We've seen this repeatedly demonstrated with every modern financial crisis through the provision of taxpayer-funded bailouts (socializing the losses of publicly-traded companies) in the name of preventing contagion. Actions made possible due to misaligned incentives created by a centralized fiat system.

Centralization usually brings along serious risks of monopolization, corruption, exclusion and abuses."

-GIACOMO ZUCCO

Bitcoin offers a return to full responsibility. Accounting for all existing units is trivial, as is enforcing the supply schedule. Favors cannot be granted, no matter the participant.

SATOSHI NAKAMOTO

"The root problem with conventional currency is all the trust that's required to make it work. The central bank must be trusted not to debase the currency, but the history of fiat currencies is full of breaches of that trust."

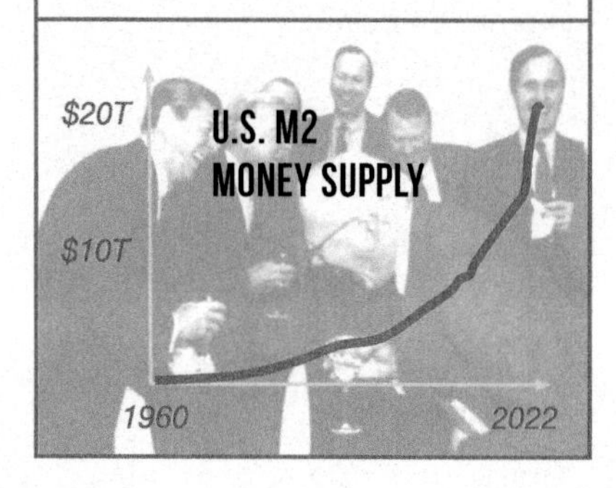

RELATED CONCEPT

COUNTERPARTY RISK

The likelihood of a party defaulting on its obligation in a transaction.

Almost all digital financial transactions today require a relationship with a regulated entity (institution, platform, or custodian). These entities act as counterparties whose role is to facilitate economic activity on behalf of customers.

The presence of a counterparty in a transaction introduces certain risks into the equation. Primarily the risk of default (failing to meet obligations of delivery or settlement). Even if the probability is relatively minor, the consequences can be catastrophic.

Unpredictable events bring rise to unexpected actions, especially in financial markets.

Trust in fiat money will always be linked to the viability of the current government as a going concern. Even if issued during a period of relative stability and perceived solvency, fiat money can always deteriorate at a future point (if not present).

Bitcoin does away with the need for an issuing authority, removing future solvency risks. As a bearer asset, it dispenses with the need for counterparties as custodians. Similarly, as a peer-to-peer network, counterparties become entirely redundant.

NIK BHATIA

"Layers become a way to think about money's natural hierarchy whereupon monetary instruments are ranked in order of superiority from top to bottom, instead of placed next to each other on accounting tables."

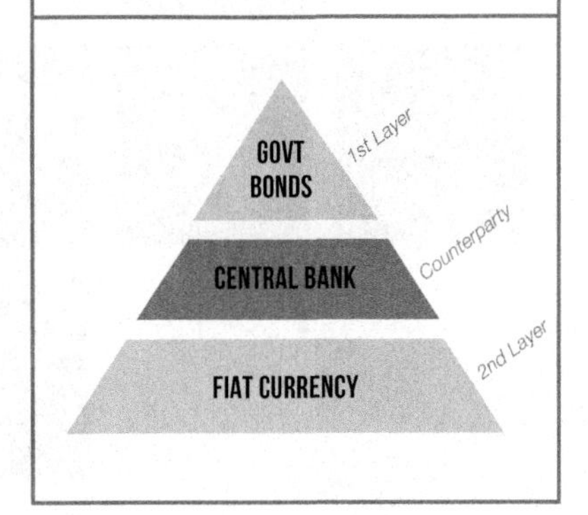

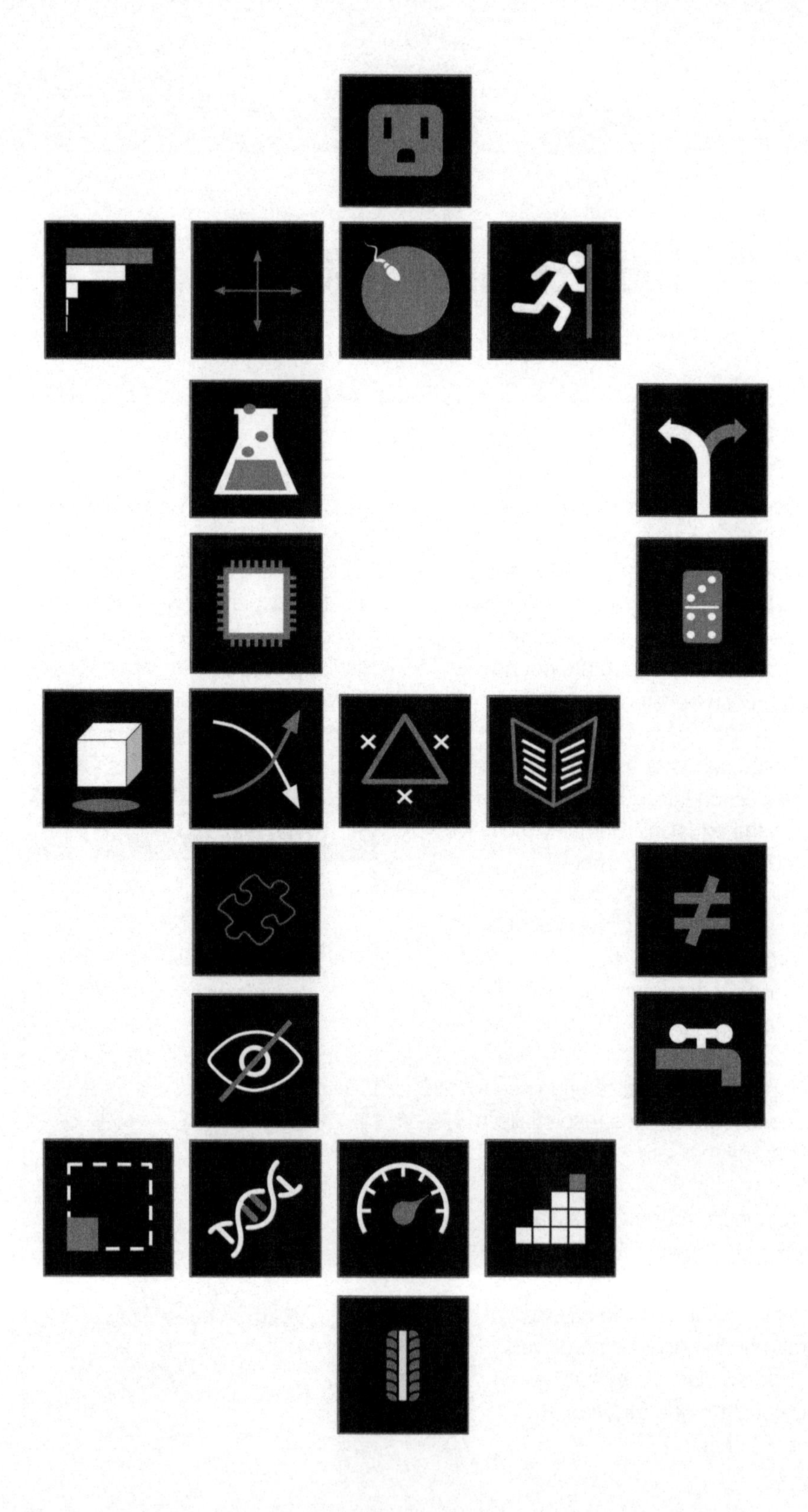

Further Reading

SCARCITY

Thomas Sowell, *"Is Reality Optional?: And Other Essays,"* 1993.
Vijay Boyapati, *"The Bullish Case for Bitcoin,"* 2018.

GRESHAM'S LAW

Robert Mundell, *"Uses and Abuses of Gresham's Law in the History of Money,"* 1998.

CANTILLON EFFECT

Richard Cantillon, *"Essai sur la Nature du Commerce en Général,"* 1755.
Jörg Guido Hülsmann, *"The Ethics of Money Production,"* 2008.

SCHELLING POINT

Nick Szabo, *"Money, Blockchains, and Social Scalability,"* 2017.
Balaji S. Srinivasan, *"Bitcoin becomes the Flag of Technology,"* 2020.

OPPORTUNITY COST

Saifedean Ammous, *"The Fiat Standard,"* 2021.

IMPOSSIBLE TRINITY

Robert Mundell, *"Capital Mobility and Stabilization Policy under Fixed and Flexible Exchange Rates,"* 1963.

JEVONS PARADOX

William Stanley Jevons, *"The Coal Question,"* 1865.
Vaclav Smil, *"Energy and Civilization: A History,"* 2017.

POWER LAWS

Parker Lewis, *"Bitcoin, Not Blockchain,"* 2019.
Lyn Alden, *"Bitcoin: Addressing Misconceptions,"* 2020.

UNIT BIAS

Vijay Boyapati, *"The Bullish Case for Bitcoin," 2018.*

VEBLEN GOOD

Thorstein Veblen, *"The Theory of the Leisure Class: An Economic Study of Institutions,"* 1899.

MALINVESTMENT

Murray Rothbard, *"Man, Economy, and State: A Treatise on Economic Principles,"* 1962.
Parker Lewis, *"Bitcoin is the Great Definancialization,"* 2020.

ASYMMETRIC PAYOFF

Howard Marks, *"I Beg to Differ,"* 2022.

ANSOFF MATRIX

Igor Ansoff, *"Strategies for Diversification,"* 1957.
Brandon Quittem, *"Bitcoin is The Mycelium of Money,"* 2020.

II

ORDERS OF MAGNITUDE

Parker Lewis, *"Bitcoin Obsoletes All Other Money,"* 2020.
Peter Thiel, *"Zero to One,"* 2014.

NETWORK EFFECTS

Timothy F. Peterson, *"Bitcoin Spreads Like a Virus,"* 2019.
Ross Stevens, *"Stoneridge Shareholder Letter,"* 2020.

FRICTION

Robert Breedlove, *"Money, Bitcoin and Time: Part 2 of 3,"* 2019.

CREATIVE DESTRUCTION

Matt Ridley, *"How Innovation Works,"* 2020.
Jeff Booth, *"The Greatest Game,"* 2020.

FEEDBACK LOOPS

Brandon Quittem, *"Bitcoin is a Catalyst for Human Evolution."* 2020.
George Soros, *"The Alchemy of Finance,"* 1987.

RELATIVITY

Vijay Boyapati, *"The Bullish Case for Bitcoin," 2018.*

THERMODYNAMICS (1ST)

Gigi, *"Bitcoin is Digital Scarcity,"* 2022.
Knut Svanholm, *"Bitcoin and Thermodynamics,"* 2018.
Nic Carter, *"It's the Settlement Assurances, Stupid,"* 2019.

THERMODYNAMICS (2ND)

Gigi, *"Bitcoin's Eternal Struggle,"* 2019.
Gigi, *"Bitcoin is Time,"* 2021.
Claude E. Shannon, "*A Mathematical Theory of Communication,"* 1949.

MOORE'S LAW

Gordon Moore, *"Cramming more components onto integrated circuits,"* 1965.

ANTIFRAGILITY

Andreas M. Antonopoulos, "*The Internet of Money (Vol. I)," 2016.*
Nik Bhatia, *"Layered Money," 2021.*
Nassim Taleb, *"Antifragile: Things That Gain From Disorder," 2012.*
Giacomo Zucco, *"Bitcoin & the HOPF Cycle of the Internet,"* 2020.

GALL'S LAW

Allen Farrington & Big Al, *"Only The Strong Survive,"* 2020.
John Gall, *"Systemantics: How Systems Work & Especially How They Fail,"* 1977.
Parker Lewis, *"Bitcoin is Not Too Slow,"* 2019.
Gigi, *"Implications of Outlawing Bitcoin,"* 2021.

CATALYSTS

Ross Stevens, *"Stoneridge Shareholder Letter,"* 2020.

PRISONER'S DILEMMA

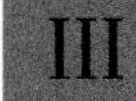

Parker Lewis, *"Bitcoin Cannot Be Banned,"* 2019.
Chris Kuiper and Jack Neureuter, *"Research Round-Up: 2021 Trends and Their Potential Future Impact,"* 2022.

SOCIAL PROOF

Luke Burgis, *"Wanting: The Power of Mimetic Desire in Everyday Life,"* 2021.

CIRCLE OF COMPETENCE

Justin Kruger & David Dunning, *"Unskilled and unaware of it: How difficulties in recognizing one's own incompetence lead to inflated self-assessments,"* 1999.

GARTNER HYPE CYCLE

Matt Ridley, *"Amara's Law,"* 2017.

INTRANSIGENT MINORITY

Nassim Taleb, *"Skin in the Game: Hidden Asymmetries in Daily Life,"* 2018.

INEQUIVALENCE THEOREM

James Davidson ve William Rees-Mogg, "*The Sovereign Individual,"* 1997.
Nick Szabo, *"Schelling Out: The Origins of Money,"* 2002.

LINDY EFFECT

Willem Van Den Bergh, *"On Schelling points, network effects and Lindy: Inherent properties of communication,"* 2018.

EMERGENCE

Saifedean Ammous, *"The Bitcoin Standard,"* 2018.
Tuur Demeester, *"The Bitcoin Reformation,"* 2019.

MORAL HAZARD

Parker Lewis, *"Bitcoin is a Rally Cry,"* 2020.
Nik Bhatia, "Layered Money," 2021.

ACKNOWLEDGEMENTS

Jeff Booth, Saifedean Ammous, Will Cole, Cristian Keroles, Giacomo Zucco, Vijay Boyapati, Cory Klippsten, Gigi, Parker Lewis, Preston Pysh, Stephan Livera, Tuur Demeester, Knut Svanholm, hodlonaut, Robert Breedlove, Brady Swenson, Wizard of Aus, and all the folks at Konsensus Publishing.

"You never change things by fighting the existing reality. To change something, build a new model that makes the existing model obsolete."

-BUCKMINSTER FULLER

Printed in Great Britain
by Amazon